I0422282

ANTECEDENTS TO WINNING THE MALCOLM BALDRIGE AWARD AND ACHIEVING SUPERIOR PERFORMANCE

Doctoral Dissertation Research

Submitted to the Graduate Faculty of Argosy University,
Washington DC Campus
Graduate School of Business and Management

In Fulfillment of
the Requirements for the Degree of Doctor of Business
Administration

by
Dr. Millie M. Stout
July, 2016

RoseDog Books

PITTSBURGH, PENNSYLVANIA 15238

ANTECEDENTS TO WINNING THE MALCOLM BALDRIGE AWARD AND ACHIEVING SUPERIOR PERFORMANCE

The contents of this work, including, but not limited to, the accuracy of events, people, and places depicted; opinions expressed; permission to use previously published materials included; and any advice given or actions advocated are solely the responsibility of the author, who assumes all liability for said work and indemnifies the publisher against any claims stemming from publication of the work.

All Rights Reserved
Copyright © 2022 by Dr. Millie M. Stout

No part of this book may be reproduced or transmitted, downloaded, distributed, reverse engineered, or stored in or introduced into any information storage and retrieval system, in any form or by any means, including photocopying and recording, whether electronic or mechanical, now known or hereinafter invented without permission in writing from the publisher.

Dorrance Publishing Co
585 Alpha Drive
Suite 103
Pittsburgh, PA 15238
Visit our website at *www.dorrancebookstore.com*

ISBN: 979-8-88604-625-0
eISBN: 979-8-88604-709-7

ANTECEDENTS TO WINNING THE MALCOLM BALDRIGE AWARD AND ACHIEVING SUPERIOR PERFORMANCE

Doctoral Dissertation Research

Submitted to the Graduate Faculty of
Argosy University, Washington DC Campus

Graduate School of Business and Management

In Partial Fulfillment of
the Requirements for the Degree of
Doctor of Business Administration

by

Dr. Millie M. Stout

July, 2022

Dissertation Committee Approval:

_____
Florence Richman, Ph.D., Chair   Date

_____
Brian Sloboda, Ph.D., Committee Member   Date

_____
Grace Klinefelter, DBA, Program Chair   Date

ABSTRACT

Business organizations believe in the authenticity and value of the Malcolm Baldrige National Quality Award (MBNQA) and strive to earn this accolade. However, the actions of organizations, in terms of time and financial expenditures, do not appear to justify the benefits from winning the MBNQA. The purpose of this quantitative correlational study was to determine if winning the MBNQA had a significant effect on firm performance, as measured by returns on assets (ROA), and the nature of the relationship between the both the number of employees in the firm and the price-to-sales ratio of the firm and the price-to-sales ratio of competing firms. Data from a sample of MBNQA winners during the period 2004-2015 were analyzed. Two hypotheses were tested and auxiliary analysis was conducted using linear regressions and dependent samples r tests. The results indicated that firms that had not won the MBNQA during the period of 2004-2015 outperformed winning firms during the same period and winning the MBNQA did not significantly affect firm ROA, ROE, EVA, or MVA. Furthermore, there was not a statistically significant difference in ROA, returns on equity (ROE), economic value added (EVA), or market value added (MVA) prior to winning the MBNQA and after winning the MBNQA. It is recommended that other researchers replicate this study with a larger sample size and limit their analysis to the performance measures of corporations in specific economic sectors.

ACKNLOWLEDGMENTS

I would like to acknowledge my dissertation program chair, Dr. Grace Kline-felter, my dissertation chair, Dr. Florence Richman, and my committee member, Dr. Brian Sloboda, for their assistance with my dissertation. It would not have been possible with their dedication. A special thanks to my husband, Aaron Stout. No matter what obstacles we faced, he continued to encourage me to work hard to complete my doctorate degree.

To my children, Felistah and Katie, for their continuing support in assisting me with chores and making life a little easier while I continued my education.

DEDICATION

This dissertation is dedicated to mother Janet and my dad Jeremiah, who I love so much, and who believed in me when I did not believe in myself.

TABLE OF CONTENTS

CHAPTER ONE: INTRODUCTION...1

Background Problem 1

Purpose of Study. 3

    Research Question...3

    Hypotheses 3

    Research Methodology. 3

    Justification for the Methodology and Statistical Analysis. 4

    Study Population and Data Collection. 5

    Analysis Tool 5

    Decision Rule 6

    Validity and Reliability..6

    Credibility of Sources of Information.......................................6

    Research Ethics..7

    Project Timeline 7

Limitations. 13

Delimitations...13

Definitions of Terms. 14

Significance of the Study...15

    The Malcom Baldrige Award. 15

    Origin off the MBNQA 18

    Theoretical Framework—

    Organizational Performance and the MBNQA Criteria...............20

CHAPTER TWO: LITERATURE REVIEW. 21

Performance Excellence...24

Dilemmas and Criticism 27

    Quality Management and Firm's Performance..........................30

    Quality Standard...31

Conclusion. 32

CHAPTER THREE: METHODOLOGY. 33

    Purpose Statement 33

    Research Question. 34

    Hypotheses. 34

    Research Methodology. 35

    Justification for the Methodology and Statistical Analysis...........37

    Study Population and Data Collection..................................38

    Analysis Tool 39

    Validity and Reliability. 39

    Conceptual Model...40

    Theoretical Model. 40

    Definition of Variables 41

    Data Collection. 43

        Sample...43

        Targets Population..45

        Inclusion Criteria..45

    Steps for NQA Winners. 47

        Data Collection Process for NQA Winners. 47

        Instrumentation. 48

        Procedures. 48

        Data Gathering. 48

        Data Analysis..48

        Limitations...49

        Delimitations 49

        Key Competitors of NQA Winners.................................49

        Performance Excellence Program (BPEP) 50

        Sources of Data...53

    Data Analysis. 54

        Statistical Approach. 54

        Testing for Normality. 54

        Validity and Reliability..55

    Ethical Considerations..58

    Summary..59

CHAPTER FOUR: RESULTS 61
    Restatement of the Purpose...61
    Description of the Sample 61
    Assumption Testing..66
    Hypothesis Testing...70
        Hypothesis 1 70
        Hypothesis 2. 71
        Auxiliary Analysis...72
        Regression Using Returns on Earnings.....................................72
        Regression Using Economic Value Added.................................73
        Regression Using Market Value Added. 74
        Dependent Samples / Tests on the
        Four Measures of Firm Performance...75
    Summary..76

CHAPTER FIVE: SUMMARY, FINDINGS, CONCLUSIONS,
AND RECOMMENDATION. 77
    Summary..77
    Conclusions. 79
    Implications for the Study, Data Processing and Analysis. 80
        Findings. 81
        Recommendations 83
        Summary...84
        Conclusions................,. 84

REFERENCES...87

LIST OF TABLES

Table 1. MBNQA Recipients by Category from 1988 to 2010...................44

Table 2. MBNQA Recipients by Category from 1999 to 2010...................44

Table 3. MBNQA Recipients Sample from 1999 to 2010...........................45

Table 4. MBNQA Recipients by Category from 2010 to 2015...................46

Table 5. Elements of Data Queries in COMPUSTAT...............................54

Table 6. Central Tendency of Number of Employees,
Price/Sales, and Competitor Price/Sales.......................................62

Table 7. Central Tendency of Returns on Assets by MBNQA
Winner During 2004-2015..62

Table 8. Central Tendency of Return on Earnings by MBNQA
Winner During 2004- 2015...63

Table 9. Central Tendency of Economic Value Added by MBNQA
Winner During 2004- 2015...64

Table 10. Central Tendency of MVA by MBNQA
Winner During 2004-2015 65

Table 11. Linear Regression Analysis Using MBNQA
Outcome to Predict ROA...70

Table 12. Linear Regression Analysis Using the Number of Employees,
Price/Sales Ratio, and Price/Sales Ratio of Competing
Firm to Predict ROA. 71

Table 13. Linear Regression Analysis Using MBNQA
Outcome to Predict ROE..73

Table 14. Linear Regression Analysis Using MBNQA
Outcome to Predict Economic Value Added. 74

Table 15. Linear Regression Analysis Using MBNQA
Outcome to Predict Market Value Added......................................75

Table 16. Dependent Samples / Tests on the Four Measures of
Firm Performance...76

LIST OF FIGURES

Figure 1. Annual comparison of stock performance between
S&P 500 and NQA winners 26

Figure 2. Frequency distribution of variables used in testing
Hypothesis 1 and Hypothesis 2 66

Figure 3. Frequency distribution of variables used in testing returns
on earnings, economic value added, and market value added.......67

Figure 4. Frequency distribution of variables used in t tests on returns
on assets, returns On Earnings, and economic value added 68

Figure 5. Frequency distribution of variables used in t test on
market value added 69

Figure 6. Scatterplot of the standardized residuals against the
standardized predicted values for the multiple linear
regression conducted to test Hypothesis 2.....................................69

CHAPTER ONE: INTRODUCTION

Background Problems

Business organizations believe in the authenticity and value of the Malcolm Baldrige National Quality Award (MBNQA) and strive to earn this prestigious accolade (Cazzell & Ulmer, 2009; Hladchenko, 2015). The MBNQA has a powerful effect on financial returns and earnings, thus, organizations are willing to spend great amounts of money and time on winning the award (Foma, 2012; Gorelick, 2004; Jacob, Madu, & Tang, 2004). However, the actions of organizations in terms of spending money and time do not paint a true picture of their performance. One such case is that of Cadillac, which received the MBNQA in 2005. One of the major deficiency of the award is its recipients' failure to reflect outstanding product quality. This decision resulted in a loss of integrity for the award. It remains crucial to measure the quality in terms of customers' perceptions and opinions and not those of the manufactures or engineers. Gorelick (2004) asserted that "it was evident in reports that Cadillac was losing market share and failed to distinguish itself in customer-satisfaction ratings — Lexus, Infiniti and other competitors had come on stronger than Cadillac" (p. 7).

A study carried out by Jacob et al. (2012) endeavored to find whether winning the MBNQA adds value to firms and their investors or not. The findings of the study suggest that winners of this award do witness an increase in market value. The study also revealed that return on equity, market value added, and return on assets are primary predictors of firm performance. Jacob et al. (2012) asserted that, "indeed, without adequate controls, it is also plausible that variables other than quality were responsible for the Baldrige Award winners' enhanced market returns" (p. 900).

1

However, Jacob et a1. (2012) did not provide statistical evidence to support how the MBNQA influences these factors. Therefore, a research gap exists that can be addressed by the findings of the present study, which will investigate the impact of winning the MBQNA on a firm's performance. This area of inquiry appears worth investigating. The intention of the MBNQA is to improve management's quality awareness and recognize outstanding accomplishments in quality product improvement as compared to other U.S. businesses. Another purpose of the award is to give other U.S. firms ideas and strategies regarding how to improve the quality of their products, therefore, all MBNQA winners are required to share their experiences publicly

There appears to be a concern that winning the MBNQA is not a measure of a firm's performance, yet the reason behind this is that companies believe the award will have a positive effect on the company's financial returns and earnings. However, the money and effort spent on the award and the cost incurred may result in a diminishment of profit and not necessarily lead to better performance. This point is strengthened through the report that Cadillac's market shares were dropping and did not surpass any other companies in customer-satisfaction ratings during the time they won the award. Cadillac was being outperformed by Infiniti, Lexus, and other competitors (Gorelick, 2004; Foma, 2012; Jacob et al., 2004).

The design for this quantitative study seeks to determine if winning the MBQNA (independent variable) results in better firm performance (dependent variable). The purpose of the award leads the researcher to believe that the winning company is the best in the return of equity, market value added, economic value added and return on assets (proxies representing dependent variable, i.e., firm performance). Although there are companies that may outperform MBNQA winning companies in some areas, the winning companies' outperform the competitors in many other areas, making them the overall winner. However, there seems to be some factors that are deemed more important than others.

Purpose of Study

The purpose of this research is to examine if winning the MBQNA (IV) has a significant effect on firm performance, as measured by returns on assets (ROA). The list of MBNQA winners in an 11-year period (2004 -2015) formed the basis of this study and did the following:

Research Question
Does winning the MBNQA have a significant effect on a Return on Assets? To answer this question, this study examined the relationship between MBNQA and ROA.

Hypotheses
A multiple regression were used to determine the effect of winning the MBNQA and the effect other variables have on the identified dependent variables (Return on Earnings). The following statistical hypotheses were be tested:

Hal: BROE # 0 where BRoE is the slope of whether the firm has won the MBQNA. That is, winning the MBQNA has a statistically significant effect on a return on earnings. Ha2: BROA # 0, where BRoA is the slope of other individual independent variables (to be identified by this study). That is, each specific variable has a statistically significant effect on a return on earnings.

Research Methodology
This was a quantitative study using a multiple regression to examine if winning the MBQNA (IV) has a significant effect on firm performance, as measured by ROA. The multiple regression is used to determine if there is a correlation between earning the MBNQA and ROA. The list of MBNQA winners in an 11-year period (2004-2015) formed the basis of this study. The research project focused on MBNQA winning companies that won and may not have earned their award through their quality or market returns. The dependent variables (DV) were the ROA for firms following the winning of a NQA. Other DVs include return of assets, market value added, economic value added, and return on equity (proxies representing dependent variable, e.g., firm performance).

Financial performance is generally represented through two parameters that include ROA and ROE. ROA is measured in terms of net income divided by total assets and has the entire focus on how a firm's profitability is relative to its total assets.

Similarly, ROE is measured in terms of net income to shareholder's equity indicating the amount of net income that is being received out of the total investment provided by shareholders in the firm.

Economic value added is the variable that measures the financial performance of an organization based on the calculated residual wealth (Priester & Wang, 2010). In the quest of creating value, multinational companies, such as General Electric, Coca Cola, Siemens, Sony, and AT&T, have already used EVA as a performance measurement tool for management system (Ray, 2010, p. 117). Tong, Yao, and Xiong (2010) stated "build a performance evaluation system based on Economic Value Added and Balanced Scorecard for logistics enterprises empirically and found that EVA gets significantly positive Kendall tau's correlation with strategic objective whose proxy is corporate value" (p. 122). Wang and Fan (2010) "presented [a] performance model based on EVA method that focus on value creation attending comprehensive measurement of service-oriented enterprises. The result showed that service center of issuing has a negative EVA although its profit is positive" (p. 122).

Market value added shows the difference between the market value of a company and the capital contributed by investors (both bondholders and shareholders). In other words, it is the sum of all capital claims held against the company plus the market value of debt and equity (Wang & Fan, 2010, p. 122).

Justification for the Methodology and Statistical Analysis

The appropriateness of the quantitative method for the current study stems from the study's goal of collecting objective, numeric data for testing associations among variables, using statistical methods (Creswell, 2008). The quantitative method is particularly useful for answering research questions related to measurement of variables, testing of theories, and prediction of outcomes (Leedy & Ormrod, 2005, 2013; Creswell, 2008; Dyer, 2006; Neuman, 2003).

Similarly, the appropriateness of the correlational design for the current study derives from the study's requirement to test associations among multiple independent variables (MBNQA) and a dependent variable (firm performance). The literature (e.g., Leedy & Ormrod, 2013; Creswell, 2008; Sproull, 2002; Tabachnick & Fiddel, 2001a) has shown that the correlational design is the most appropriate quantitative approach for examining associations among variables, without inferring causality.

Study Population and Data Collection

The population under examination was the NQA firms and a random selection of NQA key competitors in similar industries over 2004-2015 period time. In order to see how Malcolm Baldrige added value to the recipients, the researcher intends to collect data from Yahoo finance articles, publicly traded articles, and other sources to search words such as antecedents to superior firm performance. The target population of the study was 100 companies that have won the MBNQA. It is impossible to target all the companies who have won MBNQAs, therefore, the participants of the survey were selected through random sampling. In this type of sampling technique, each of the population elements has an equal chance of being selected in the sample (Fowler, 2009).

Data was collected using secondary source data and was entered into SPSSTM (Statistical Package for the Social Sciences) software for analysis using a multivariate regression. In performing the research, the research material was collected from the Internet, publicly traded journals, ProQuest, EBSCOhost, and peer reviewed journals as sources of information. This study used an 11-year period of data collection (2004-2015) and a sample from 100 companies that are recipients of the award. Secondary data gather more valuable data than may be gained by limited research. Secondary research provides the latest theoretical and academic information about the ten companies investigated and it provides evidence to support the research. This would be obtained from graphs, tables, or opinions made based on a collection of previous data enabling the writer to understand and analyze what others have written on the subject (NIST, 2010).

Analysis Tool

The analysis was carried out in accordance with the responses of the secondary data from previous studies and analyzed by the means of statistical software SPSS. The next step was to input data on the computer and perform statistical analysis, interpret data, and make recommendations.

The independent variables were run in a linear regression against specific dependent variables (financial performance) resulting in a correlation (Pearson's R) that indicates the overall strength of association between the independent variables and the dependent variable, the Coefficient of Determination (R-squared) indicating the proportion of variation in the dependent variables explained by the independent variables, and slope (or coefficient B) depicting that the actual effect each independent variable has on the dependent variable. A comparison of the slopes with R-squared indicated which independent variables have the greatest effect and to what extent.

Decision Rule

Hypotheses were tested at the o = .05 level. If the slope B for any specific independent variable does not equal '0' and the p-value is less than .05, then the null hypothesis for that independent variable can be rejected.

Validity and Reliability

The data for this study was raw data from recognized and established data collection institutions, such as the Bureau of Labor Statistics. No data collection instrument was used or designed for this specific study and the validity of the data was assumed to be robust.

Credibility of Sources of Information

Researchers describe data as the mass of disordered, raw material from which knowledge (Information) is abstracted to furnish evidence to support arguments and conclusions (Creswell, 2013). Information system technologists have adopted a similar distinction by defining information as processed data sets attaining meaning. Information instructs and evidence supports conclusions (Creswell, 2013). While neither information nor evidence is self-evident, the material seldom speaks for itself. In order for the sources of information to be rational, interpretation is required. In 2001, De Vaus results indicated that

However, when interpretation is re-interpreted, some distortion of the original is inevitable. So, some distinctions, criteria and tests are useful to weed out distortions and 'untruths.' The distinctions adopted are between primary and secondary sources of information. The criteria used are validity, reliability, and accuracy. The main test adopted is triangulation. (p. 73)

Research Ethics

This research was conducted so that the integrity of the companies used is maintained and conflicting effects that could undermine the promise for future research are avoided. According to Creswell (2013), care must be taken to ensure that the study participants bear no risk as a result of participating in the collection of data on their respective firms. Moreover, all the secondary material included in the study was properly in-texted and cited by the specific author's name and year of publication to identify and authenticate sources. All Argosy University human factors guidelines for conducting research shall be followed.

Project Timeline

The project timeline would run in accordance with the rules and regulations of the institution. First, presentation of the proposal becomes the first section of the project.

This was supposed to take a time period of two weeks where all the planning of the sections, as indicated in the proposal, was done. Once approved, the second part involved the drawing up of a dissertation based on the proposal as the background. Secondary sources were collected to complement the literature review. This was supposed to take one month as it is a most rigorous section. Once all the data are collected, writing of the dissertation commenced and took four months since the information collected has to be strategically analyzed.

In order to attain ultimate success in a competitive business environment, quality management remains an indispensable component that needs to be incorporated in an organization's overall business strategy. Any firm can lose its competitive advantage and business if it is not able to produce high quality goods and services (Kotler, 2000; Kotter, 2012). Several studies have confirmed the correlation between a firm's competitive advantage and quality management and process improvements initiatives (Chong & Rundus, 2004; Kotler, 2000; Kotter, 2012). This relationship demonstrates the importance of understanding, in detail, the link between business performances and quality improvement initiatives, specifically for National Quality Award (NQA) firms.

Elements of quality, such as customer satisfaction, return on assets, defect rates, and cycle times, informs current understanding of what quality management should entail (Griffith et al., 2012).

A number of firms have shifted their focus to quality and process improvement initiatives in order to remain in the competitive marketplace. Wilson, Walsh, and Needy (2003) stated that, "approximately 60 programs and awards reward firms for improving quality globally" (p. 3). One of the most prestigious awards for quality management is the NQA, which brings value to the organization. Extending the influence of NQA, 37 state governments have emulated the NQA and its evaluative structure (The Alliance for Performance Excellence, 2008). The Alliance for Performance Excellence (2008) serves as a clearinghouse for information about NQA. It is "a nonprofit network of international, national, state, and local Baldrige-based award programs. Members of The Alliance contribute over $30 million annually to economic competitiveness by assisting organizations in all industries on their journey to excellence" (para. 2).

A range of methods can be used to measure business performance. In this respect, the MBNQA recognizes the excellence of non-profit, health care, and business sectors.

The award came into effect after being signed by President Ronald Reagan in 1987. The award is administered by the National Institute of Standards and Technology (NIST, 2011). The purpose of this award is to encourage management's focus on customer satisfaction through quality. The MBNQA is considered a highly significant contributor in transforming U.S. business through increased competitiveness using the model of improved overall quality.

The principle on which the MBNQA is based is that of total quality management (TQM). Under this principle, the organization has to enhance its overall competitiveness level by continuously improving its performance. The issue in adoption of TQM is that it needs a long-term strategic orientation instead of short-term initiatives. For this reason it is important that the workforce as a whole is motivated to achieve quality standards and improve those standards continuously. A high level of participation from all of the organization's stakeholders ensures that the company is able to implement the TQM model effectively. Without the complete participation of the relevant organizational stakeholders, the company would fail to achieve positive performance related results.

This lack of participation is a potential issue among the companies that seek to adopt the TQM model of other organizations without adequately conducting an internal and external analysis (Brooks, 2005).

The previous discussion of the MBNQA reveals how the award affects the quality performance of the organizations as well as the criteria for the award. The background clearly shows the need to assess the performance-based issues that American companies face in striving to attain the MBNQA (Beard & Humphrey, 2014). For this purpose, the implementation of the TQM model and its role in management needs to be analyzed so the organizations can adopt the methods and strategies for achieving the prestigious M8QNA.

There appears to be a concern that winning the Malcolm Baldrige Award is not a measure of a firm performance, however, companies spend large amount of resources, money, and time in pursuit of the award, believing the MBQNA has a positive effect on competitive advantage. Should winning the MBQNA award be a measure of a firm's higher performance, such as higher ROA? There is some evidence that the cost incurred and the effort spent by companies to win the award may actually result in diminished earnings and not necessarily lead to better performance as expected. This study areas is strengthened by the fact that other studies have shown mixed results. According to Van der Laan, Van Ees, and Van Witteloostuijn (2008),

(A)nalysis of firm's social performance indicates that meeting the wider interests of stakeholders with a close connection to the firm is associated with higher performance as measured by return on assets and earnings-per-share. In contrast, higher performance on Dimensions of interest to secondary stakeholders has not translated into higher financial performance. (p. 8)

Sabella, Kashou, and Omran (2014) suggested that there is no clear and convincing evidence that winning the MBNQA results in higher performance. Some firms that do not win the MBNQA might outperform their competitors in other areas, making them all winners in terms of quality and performance outcomes. This study attempted to answer the question of whether winning the MBQNA is a measure of a firm's higher performance, such as higher ROA.

Several studies have investigated how quality implementation practices within a firm impact its financial performance. Foster (2007) found a positive correlation between quality practices and stock value in 108 firms. Howard, Foster, and Shannon (2005) used the winning of a quality award as a proxy for effective implementation of TQM. In their research, they found strong evidence that winners of quality awards outperformed control firms on operating-income-based measures. In another study, prediction of performance was considered best in the return on earnings (ROE), market value added (MVA), economic value added (EVA) and return on assets (ROA), as factors deemed proxies for a firm's performance (Jacob et al., 2012).

Jacob et al. (2012) suggested
(T)hat award winners do witness an increase in market value. By and large, the authors feel that when all the benefits of the Baldrige Performance Excellence Program are considered and given the short-term focus of studies in this area, the elimination of the program would be a terrible mistake. (p. 897)

This study attempted to address whether winning the MBNQA improves firm's performance that have won the MBNQA between 2004-2015 by examining the factors that contribute to winning the MBNQA and the linkages between quality improvement initiatives and company performance, particularly among firms that have won. It is possible that by processing a good understanding of both company performance and antecedents to winning the MBNQA, leaders might see competitive advantage and performance as the basis for their quality strategy.

The purpose of this research is to examine if winning the MBQNA (independent variable [IV]) has a significant effect on firm performance as measured by ROA. Several accesses can be used to establish the performance of economic and financial organizations. Because of the simplicity of the calculations involved, in this study the researcher opted for the use of ROA. There is an issue with the use of turnover as a measure of organizational performance because it is not used by all organizations. There is an additional issue associated with the use of this particular metric due to the difficulty of linking the concept of turnover with the performance award as a whole. The results of such an attempt would be less tangible and would not allow for a direct numerical value. It is for this reason that this researcher opted to use ROA as the primary focus as opposed to the ROE of the organization.

Hermes, Melo, and Negrao (2008) stated, when choosing the performance indicator, it is necessary to take into account the efficiency of the calculation in order to achieve the proposed objectives. In this sense, one of the most common indicators that was used in this study was ROA.

EVA is the variable that measures the financial performance of an organization based on the calculated residual wealth (Priester & Wang, 2010). Stem (1993), Stewart (1991), and Priester and Wang (2010) suggested that the EVA indicator has been extensively used in the accounting literature. The concept of EVA originated in the microeconomic literature and has tried to describe a link between a firm's earnings and shareholders' wealth creation. It is an indicator used to measure economic profit. EVA is the result of subtracting the opportunity cost of invested capital from the net operating profit after tax. The opportunity cost can be determined by multiplying the weighted average cost of debt and equity capital by the amount of capital employed. Stem and Stewart argued that, unlike some other performance indicators such as earnings per share (EPS) or earnings before interest, taxes, depreciation, and amortization (EBITDA), EVA gauges both operating and financial activities. Stem and Stewart suggested that companies that apply EVA in their performance measurement can use several methods to increase this indicator and their performance (Priester & Wang, 2010; as listed below to increase this indicator).

- Improving the net operating profit after tax generated by existing capital.
- Reducing the debt or equity capital employed.
- Investing in potential projects where the ROI of this investment exceeds the weighted average cost of capital.
- Divesting capital where the ROI of the project is less than the weighted average cost of capital.

In a comparative study, Haddad (2012) contrasted intellectual capital with EVA. For example, in terms of financial representation, he argued that EVA ties financial calculation and risk with investment indicators. However, the financial and non-financial indicators are loosely tied with invested capital (IC) from an IC perspective. With respect to growth, future growth is based on capital and cost structures of the firm from an EVA perspective. However, future growth is a representation of human, organizational, and relational capital development from an IC perspective. For EVA, strategies are determined based on the net present value calculation. For IC, strategies are determined based on the need to increase productivity and creativity. Therefore, the objectives for the two measurement methods are different. Brigham and Ehrhardt (2013) argued that although the EVA method was not developed to measure the value of intangible assets, several intellectual capital studies have discussed it when reviewing the methods to measure IC.

Although the previous literature suggested EVA might be used as an indicator to measure the flow of IC, Brigham and Ehrhardt (2013) questioned the appropriateness of this indicator in measuring the value added of intangible resources. As evidenced by Stem (1993), Stewart (1991) suggested indicators might outperform some traditional financial performance in measuring wealth. However, it does not separate wealth creation into tangible and intangible sources.

In the quest for creating value, multinational companies such as General Electric, Coca Cola, Siemens, Sony, and AT&T have already used EVA as a performance measurement tool for management system (Ray, 2010). Tong et al. (2010) have "constructed a performance evaluation system based on Economic Value Added and Balanced Scorecard for logistics enterprises empirically and found that EVA gets significantly positive Kendall tau's correlation with strategic objective whose proxy is corporate value" (p. 122). Wang and Fan (2010) "presented a performance model based on EVA method that focus on value creation attending comprehensive measurement of service-oriented enterprises. The result showed that service center of issuing has a negative EVA although its profit is positive" (p. 122).

MVA shows the difference between the market value of a company and the capital contributed by investors (both bondholders and shareholders). In other words, it is the sum of all capital claims held against the company plus the market value of debt and equity (Wang & Fan, 2010).

Limitations

The methodology of this study was influenced by many conditions and shortcomings that are not under this researcher's control. The first limitation of the study lies in the data analysis method that is based purely on statistical results. As a company's financial performance, particularly ROA, is to be judged based on MBNQA, it would have been useful to incorporate interviews of the participants to anticipate the influence of financial performance given the resources and limitations of the organization. Another limitation is the nature of the research sample, which consists of 100 companies. Due to the nature of self-reporting, the results can be distorted based on participants' incomplete understanding of the research questions or their lack of time and attention. Also, the sample is reduced in terms of years of performance data and sector. Lastly, the researcher lacks expertise in conducting a research project, which could affect the results given time constraints and pressure to complete of study.

Delimitations

The current study intends to examine only those firms that have won a MBNQA from 2004-2015. However, some firms were eliminated from consideration because of their incomplete company records. It is important that organizational performance data be available five years before and five years after winning the award for a period of 11 years. The examining company data across this 11-year time span allowed for a comparison of performance before and after winning the MBNQA. Thus, the organizations that have received awards only recently were excluded from the study due to lack of sufficient data.

Another study delimitation is the exclusion of educational and health services organizations in order to limit the scope of the study to the financial dimensions only. However, manufacturing and for-profit organizations are included as the benefits derived from improvement. These types of corporations are different from the previously mentioned sectors. Educational and health services have a diverse number of stakeholders for whom the valuation metrics might not be the same.

Definitions of Terms

Categories: This term is used to divide the evaluation criteria for MBNQA broadly for performance excellence. For example, leadership is one category.

Examiners: These are the individuals who evaluate the Baldrige application narrative and later visit the site to carry out an official examination. These individuals are trained to assess applications for the award. They evaluate the MBNQA criteria or performance excellence and also investigate any other improvements suggested by the organizations for achieving success (Bailey, 2011).

Feedback Report: The examiners generate such reports after visiting a site in which all the key business factors and themes are listed based on the organizational profile. The report also includes the comments made based on the strengths and opportunities for improvement (OFIs). The report highlights the ways in which the organization can improve by aligning itself more with MBNQA criteria for performance excellence.

Malcolm Baldrige National Quality Award (MBNQA): The business evaluation program run by the U.S. Department of Commerce's National Institute of Standards and Technology (NIST) and a private foundation since 1987. The program operates under the Malcolm Baldrige National Improvement Act (Jacob et al., 2012).

Malcolm Baldrige National Quality Criteria for Performance Excellence: This is the set of guidelines that focuses on strengthening organizations' global competitiveness by constant adoption of the latest practices for organizational effectiveness.

Quality Control: The application of the activities and techniques that are part of quality assurance (QA) that are incorporated for achieving and maintaining the product, process, or service quality.

Quality Management: The process of defining the objectives for optimal quality, developing plans for meeting those objectives, deploying the plans, and measuring their successful implementation.

Significance of the Study

The purpose of this study is to assess the impacts of winning the MBNQA on a firm's performance. The results of this study added significance to the level of understanding about the MBNQA, factors for winning it, and its impact on performance. This study had implications for both academic and management practices. Although a range of studies in the past have focused on the attributes of this award, this particular study is unique in the sense that it would furnish an understanding about how winning MBNQA can improve performance measures such as ROE, MVA, economic value, and ROA.

The Malcom Baldrige Award

There are many approaches for measuring a firm's performance. The MBNQA signed into effect by President Ronald Reagan in 1987 and administered by the National Institute of Standards and Technology recognizes performance excellence in business, health care, education, and nonprofit sectors (MBNQA, n.d.; NIST, 2010). Its purpose is to encourage management to focus on quality and customer satisfaction. Signed into law by President Ronald Reagan, the MBNQA has been viewed as a significant contributor in the transformation of U.S. businesses, particularly as a model for improving the overall quality and competitiveness of firms.

However, from the beginning, there have been arguments about the financial importance of winning the award. One reason for questioning the merits of the MBNQA is the legitimacy and accuracy of the judging process. Companies such as Cadillac, Motorola, Federal Express, and Wallace Company have never won any top ratings in quality or customer satisfaction surveys, even though it could be argued that these companies have at one time, or another maintained or failed to maintain higher quality and competitiveness over their competitors. Second, financial performance is supposed to be a factor, but many of these companies fall short of excellence. For instance,

Wallace Company of Houston, Texas, faced bankruptcy one year after winning the MBNQA. Third, many feel that the award can be essentially bought by large companies because there is no limit to how many applications a company can submit. Case in point, Xerox in 1987 and Corning in 1989 both spent over $800,000 and 14,000 hours in preparing applications for submission. Furthermore, many more hours and resources were spent coaching employees for the required site evaluations by Baldrige examiners (Jacob et al., 2004; Verhoef & Leeftang, 2009).

Being considered the highest award for quality in the United States, this researcher believes that the MBNQA not only gives praise to the deserving companies, but also provides a goal for every company to strive improve their services and products.

While criticism points out that some companies are stronger in some areas, they fail to see the overall picture and base their assumptions without all of the facts. Furthermore, the award is almost kept a secret where very few people have heard of the award or know how to apply. According to Foma (2012), only 15 companies out of the millions in the

U.S. applied for the award because they thought that the award was solely for manufacturers when that is not the case.

The law states that all Baldrige winners are required to publicly share their experiences. The award gives other US firms ideas and strategies in improving their services and products (Cazzell & Ulmer, 2009; Choi, Garcia, & Friedrich, 2009; Mena & Hult, 2009; Jacob et al., 2004; Scaraboto, 2009; Verhoef & Leeflang, 2009). According to Garvin (1991), it not only gives a clear classification of quality management principles, but also gives companies a "comprehensive framework for assessing their progress toward the new paradigm of management and such commonly acknowledged goals as customer satisfaction and increased employee involvement" (p. 93)

The MBNQA consists of various challenging performance-based criteria which have to be adequately attained by the companies in order to effectively qualify. The multidimensional criteria which are present for the award are based on various fundamental organizational attributes, hence the companies have to make a significant amount of change in order to achieve this qualification. Although a significant amount of research has been conducted regarding the overall impact of the MBNQA on the performance of the organizations, the majority of the companies still value the national award and strive to achieve qualification.

The management cannot seek to completely adopt the performance management model of another company without making the relevant changes per the internal organizational factors. This is the major dilemma which the majority of the organizations in the business industries face as they seek to attain the MBNQA. The management of some companies do not adequately analyze the internal organizational analysis and they fail to decipher the TQM requirements of their respective company. The internal analysis provides the managers with a strategic direction and the performance issues which have to be bolstered. Some organizations become dependent on the adopted benchmark model. This is a dilemma provided by the lack of internal organizational analysis conducted by the management prior to the implementation of the TQM initiative (Griffith et al., 2012).

The MBNQA is based on the principle of TQM in which the company has to continuously bolster its performance related attributes and enhancement of the overall level of competitiveness. TQM is not a short-term initiative which the company can implement without developing a long-term strategic orientation. In this approach, the management of the company has to ensure that it can motivate the overall workforce of the company to improve the quality standards. The high the level of participation from all of the organizational stakeholders, ensures that the company is able to implement the TQM model effectively. Without the complete participation of the relevant organizational stakeholders, the company would fail to achieve the positive performance related results. This is an issue created among the companies seeking to adopt the TQM model of other organizations without adequately conducting an internal and external analysis. This study would analyze the performance based issues that the American companies face in the attainment of the MBNQA (Beard & Humphrey, 2014). There are various factors the management of the companies have to critically analyze before they are able to effectively implement the TQM model and eventually achieve the prestigious Baldrige performance award.

Origin of the MBNQA

The MBNQA was signed into effect by President Ronald Reagan in 1987 and administered by the National Institute of Standards and Technology recognizes performance excellence in business, health care, education, and nonprofit sectors (MBNQA, n.d.; NIST, 2010). Its purpose is to encourage management to focus on quality and customer satisfaction. Signed into law by President Ronald Reagan, the MBNQA has been viewed as a significant contributor in the transformation of U.S. businesses, particularly as a model for improving the overall quality and competitiveness of firms (NIST 2010).

The requirements for this national level award were created by the emphasis of the U.S. Government to enhance the efficiency of the various industries, such as agricultural, pharmaceutical, and other manufacturing industries. The U.S. Government highlighted the growing emphasis of the globalization phenomena and its impact on the national business environment (Wilson & Collier, 2000; Leedy & Ormrod, 2013). The MBNQA was created to provide the American businesses with the guidelines and the criteria to become more competitive in the national business environment and also the international business market.

There are two main impacts of the MBNQA on the American business environment. The primary factor is the enhancements of the competitive framework in the national business environment, where the companies are able to enhance their operational activities (NIST, 2010). In addition, the award is provided to the companies which are able to achieve excellence in the field of manufacturing and the production capabilities, creating a challenging benchmark for the rest of the competitive forces. This enhancement in the overall level of competition has a positive impact on the growth of the national business environment and the overall quality standards present in the American business environment. The second factor of the MBNQA is the enhancement of the level of international competitiveness (Curkovic, Melnyk, Calantone, & Handheld, 2000). Moreover, the award was created as a direct result of the increasing level of globalization and its impact on the American business environment.

One of the factors to consider regarding the MBNQA qualification criteria is the fundamental changes the companies have to make in order to become eligible for this award. Although the task of attaining this challenging performance award is very difficult for the companies and can require substantial investments, the majority of the organizational entities are still motivated to qualify. The short-term benefit of attaining the MBNQA is the recognition achieved in the industry and the overall business environment (Peng & Prybutok, 2014). The MBNQA is a prestigious performance related award which highlights the core operational strengths of the company. Therefore, the achievement of these awards has a direct impact on the short-term performance of the company, and this can be identified as an objective for the management of the various organizations.

However, the short-term benefits are not the primary objective for the managements of the various organizations to seek to achieve this prestigious performance related qualification. In order to achieve the MBNQA, the companies have to make a full-time commitment to the principle of TQM and change its core ideology. This is not a small change in the organizational environment, and the organization has to ensure that it is capable of handling the major changes that it would have to make in order to qualify for the MBNQA. The performance related changes that the companies have to make in order to qualify for this award have a significant impact on the quality standards and the operational efficiency of the organization (Duarte, Goodson, & Dougherty, 2014). The primary reason why the majority of the companies seek to fulfil the core criteria of the MBNQA were the positive impact it had on the performance of the company. This attainment of the award is a long-term initiative the management of the organization has to commit to and by developing core performance, related objectives.

Through this incremental and persistent investment made by the management of the company regarding the TQM initiatives and the performance related standards of the company, the organization can become eligible for the prestigious MBNQA (Duarte et al., 2014). There has been a significant amount of research conducted on the impact of the organizational performances. Since the majority of companies present in the various industries in the U.S. have to make a significant investment in the change initiatives in order to achieve the MBNQA, the organizational management strives to conduct a costs benefit analysis of this process. Various research activities have highlighted a clear impact of the MBNQA attained by the organizations, and the enhancement of the operational performance of the companies (Peng & Prybutok, 2014). It is due to these performance related factors that the majority of the companies strive to attain the MBNQA, and enhance their competitiveness in the overall business environment.

Theoretical Framework—Organizational Performance and the MBNQA Criteria

The Malcolm Bridge criteria provide a common communication for the companies presently in the U.S. to highlight their operational and performance related strengths. The MBNQA identifies the excellence that the American companies have been able to achieve and it can be utilized as a performance related benchmark in the relevant industry. The criteria for the MBNQA are specifically designed for the companies to critically analyze their performance management systems and highlight the strengths and the opportunities which are present in the workplace environment. The secondary relation between the performance management attributes of the companies and the MBNQA criteria is that the qualified organizations can serve as role models for the rest of the American companies present in the industry (Lee, Ooi, Chong, & Seow, 2014).

The MBNQA criteria are strictly related to the concept of TQM, and it is not limited to any specific industry or type of organization. The overall performance impact of the MBNQA in the American business environment is that it leads to enhancement in the national level of business competitiveness. The companies across the various industries can seek to benchmark the organizations which are able to achieve this challenging performance related award, and the performance quality standards of the overall business environment increase. The MBNQA also promotes the innovation and creativity in the performance management systems which are implemented by the various organizations (Jacob et al., 2012). The overall objective of the national award is to enhance the performance quality standards of the companies. It is a continuous process. Based on the principle of TQM, the MBNQA criteria cause the companies to continuously strive to enhance the performance related attributes and become more competitive in nature.

CHAPTER TWO: LITERATURE REVIEW

This chapter presents an analysis of previous literature done on the MBNQA. The purpose of this study is to examine if winning the MBQNA has a significant effect on firm performance as measured by ROA. The population under examination is a set of firms whose performance was tracked both five years before and five years after receiving this award. The desired outcome of this research was to develop a theory for superior firm performance and understanding product quality and customer satisfaction.

Since its inception, the MBNQA has been viewed as a significant contributor to the transformation of U.S. businesses, particularly as a model for improving the overall quality and competitiveness of firms (National Institution of Standards and Technology, 2011). The MBNQA is awarded to firms that have enhanced the efficiency of U.S. agricultural, private sector, pharmaceutical, and other manufacturing industries. This award fosters company growth and development, essential to the survival of U.S. business and increasing the global market.

Quality management is a concept that integrates process, quality, and customer orientations. The requirements of an integrative management concept are covered by TQM. An international standard of quality was accepted through the revisions and development of the standard family International Organization for Standardization (ISO) 9000 in order to develop, implement, and satisfy a quality management system. The continuous improvement process can never be finished, but process-oriented quality management can further develop through evaluating past long-term development (Stracke, 2006). Quality will always be a complicated, yet critical factor for success in future management. The MBNQA provided U.S. businesses guidelines to become more competitive in the national business environment as well as the international business market.

The award is provided to companies that are able to demonstrate and achieve excellence in the fields of manufacturing and production, thereby creating a challenging benchmark for the rest of the firms in the award category. Revenue, cash flow, and margins are financial targets that can be included in the financial perspective. For instance, through price benchmarks, quality checks, delivery time measures, customer satisfactions evaluation, and a value proposition, metrics can be used to ensure excellence (Kaplan & Norton, 1996). By extension, the winning firm establishes quality factors that become the industry's competitive forces. When firms compete, they innovate and enhance the industry's standards for best practices standards. Any enhancement in the overall level of competition has a positive impact on the growth of the national business environment and the overall quality standards present in the American business environment (Kerzner, 2010). Another factor of the MBNQA is the enhancement of U.S. firms' international competitiveness (Curkovic et a1., 2000; Stracke, 2006).

In order to improve the quality of service, financial measures can be used to measure and then define potential strategies to minimize variation. Various performance measures have been used to quantify the impact of ISO certification on organizational and operational performance (Bell & Omachonu, 2011). Other factors that seem to affect company performance include the implementation of other quality management systems, such as ISO 14001 or 22000 (Kafetzopoulos, Gotzamani, & Psomas, 2013; To, Lee, & Yu, 2012).

The Baldrige Improvement Act states that all Baldrige winners are required to share their experiences publicly. Indeed, a key purpose of the award is to give other U.S. firms ideas and strategies for improving their services and products (Cazzell & Ulmer, 2009; Choi et a1., 2009; Jacob et al., 2004; Mena & Hult, 2009; Scaraboto, 2009; Verhoef & Leeflang, 2009). One of the factors to consider regarding the MBNQA qualification criteria is the fundamental changes companies have to make in order to become eligible for this award. This award is the recognition achieved in the industry and the overall business environment. The MBNQA is a prestigious performance related award that highlights the core operational strengths of a company. Therefore, the achievement of receiving this award has a direct impact on the company's short-term performance, which can be identified as an objective for the management of the organizations that strive to achieve the award (Peng & Prybutok, 2014).

These short-term benefits are not the primary objective for the organizations that seek to achieve this prestigious performance related distinction. In order to achieve the MBNQA, companies have to make a full-time commitment to the principle of TQM and change their core ideology. This organizational change is not a minor one; moreover, the competing companies have to ensure they are capable of handling the major changes that would have to be made in order to qualify for the MBNQA. The performance elated changes that the companies have to make in order to qualify for this award have a significant impact on quality standards and the operational efficiency of the respective organizations (Duarte et al., 2014). Performance improvement is the primary reason the majority of winning companies seek to fulfill the criteria of the MBNQA, because the initiative would have a positive impact on the performance of the company. The attainment of the award involves a long-term initiative for the managements of the organizations. This commitment requires developing core performance related factors, such as a performance excellence programs. The goal of this program is to foster U.S. innovation and industrial competitiveness by advancing measurement science, standards, and technology through an active public-private partnership (National Institution of Standards and Technology, 2011).

Through this incremental and persistent investment made by management regarding the TQM initiatives and the company's performance related standards, the organization can become eligible for the prestigious MBNQA (Duarte et al., 2014). An important factor to consider regarding this award qualification criteria is the fundamental changes the companies have to make in order to become eligible for this award.

Although the task of earning this challenging performance excellence award is very difficult for the companies and can require substantial investments, the majority of organizational entities are still motivated to qualify. The short-term benefit of attaining the MBNQA is the recognition achieved in the industry and overall business environment. According to Peng and Prybutok (2014), a clear impact of earning the MBNQA is the enhancement of the operational performance and profitability. In summary, the companies that attain the award enhance their competitiveness in the overall business environment.

According to Cazzell and Ulmer (2009) and many other experts, the process of applying for the award enables the companies to do the assessment. Tong et al. (2010) also reported three primary purposes of the MBNQA: (a) it generated effectiveness; (b) strengthened the competitiveness of the U.S business; and (c) improved the capabilities, practices, and results of organizational performance.

The primary purpose of the MBNQA is to strengthen the competitiveness of U.S. businesses by improving the capabilities, practices, and results of organizational performance. Additionally, the award is intended to facilitate communication by sharing best practice information among different types of organizations in the U.S. and to serve as a working tool to understand and manage performance on basis of organizational planning (Jacob et al., 2004; University of Wisconsin, 2011).

Performance Excellence

According to Peng and Prybutok (2014), "the MBNQA Criteria for Performance Excellence is a powerful set of guidelines for operating an effective organization and they emphasizes the need to proactively adopt the criteria if the organization's goal is performance improvement" (p. 15). According to Peng and Prybutok, the criteria and not the perspective are important when considering integration of performance management within the organization. The criteria for MBNQA are developed in a manner that results in delivering ever-improving value to the customer. Therefore, it is possible to yield improvement in overall capabilities and effectiveness of the organization along with improved quality, thereby fostering personal and organizational learning. Priester and Wang (2010) pointed out that a strength of the MBNQA is its ability to develop greater customer loyalty and produce a higher quality product or service. Risvank (2010) noted that the MBNQA encourages aligning the vision, mission, and values of the organization with its overall strategy. When defining and implementing such a strategy, Risvank noted that it is important to assess the overall performance, which is not possible without the active support and involvement of senior leadership.

The MBNQA criteria provides a common platform for U.S. companies to highlight their operational and performance related strengths. The MBNQA is an indicator of excellence and is used as a performance benchmark in the industry. The criteria for the MBNQA are the internal organizational and external organizational context, the strategic planning process, action plan development, deployment, results, and performance measurements. These components are specifically designed for companies to critically analyze their performance management systems and highlight the strengths and the opportunities present in the workplace environment. The secondary relationship between performance excellence and the MBNQA criteria is that qualified organizations can serve as role models for other companies in the industry (Lee et al., 2014). The MBNQA also promotes innovation and creativity in the performance management (Jacob et al., 2012).

Verhoef and Leeflang (2009) and Wang (2013) highlighted that as soon as the MBNQA winners are announced, the winning organizations experience an increase in stock price on the same day. Additionally, when the MBNQA is awarded, workforce engagement level is enhanced, leading to an improved rate of customer and employee satisfaction. Wang and Fan (2010) also reported that winning the MBNQA can substantially improve an organization's market share. Duarte et al. (2013) reviewed the performance of organizations that received the award previously and found they received special benefits, such as an increased pace of improvement and validation of the key results. Griffith et a1. (2012) found that the real payoff of earning the award derives from rigorous and systematic self-assessment processes and identification of performance gaps delineating areas of improvement. According to Nulla (2013), the key reasons that led to such an increase in performance is the criteria for performance excellence enables organizations to focus on their operations by identifying ways they can be improved, thus leading to a viable future. Also, organizations are able to determine the ways to address inquiries and create effective solutions to overcome performance gaps. In addition, the organization is able to develop strategic planning based on structure that allows for the analysis of the organizational system in one document (Jacob et al., 2004; Mena & Hult, 2009; Scaraboto, 2009; Verhoef & Leeflang, 2009). The ability to track organizational performance through one document allows the organization to improve further as it lends clarity and coordination to its efforts.

Winning the MBNQA directly leads to increased company profitability. Risvank (2010) conducted a study on the performance of MBNQA winners from 1988 to 1997 and found that the winners outperformed the S&P 500 by almost three to one. Based on the increased performance returns, many long-term investors also prefer to invest in Baldrige winners, as they believe the enhance shareholder, customer, and employee support to contribute to financial success.

There are benefits in following up on the value-adding capability of winning a MBNQA. Between 1995 and 2004, the MBNQA program released annual comparisons of publicly traded MBNQA recipients compared to the S&P 500. This comparison is known as the Baldrige Index. However, the practice of annually computing the Baldrige Index was discontinued in 2004. Among the reasons for the discontinuation of the annual comparisons was that an increasing number of applicants were not publicly traded companies. The MBNQA program is "currently researching alternatives to the stock study and hopes to replace it with an index that better reflects the performance of all recent Award recipients" ("NQA Stock Studies," 2008, p .2). The following is a summary of the annual comparisons of stock performance of the S&P companies and MBNQA recipients.

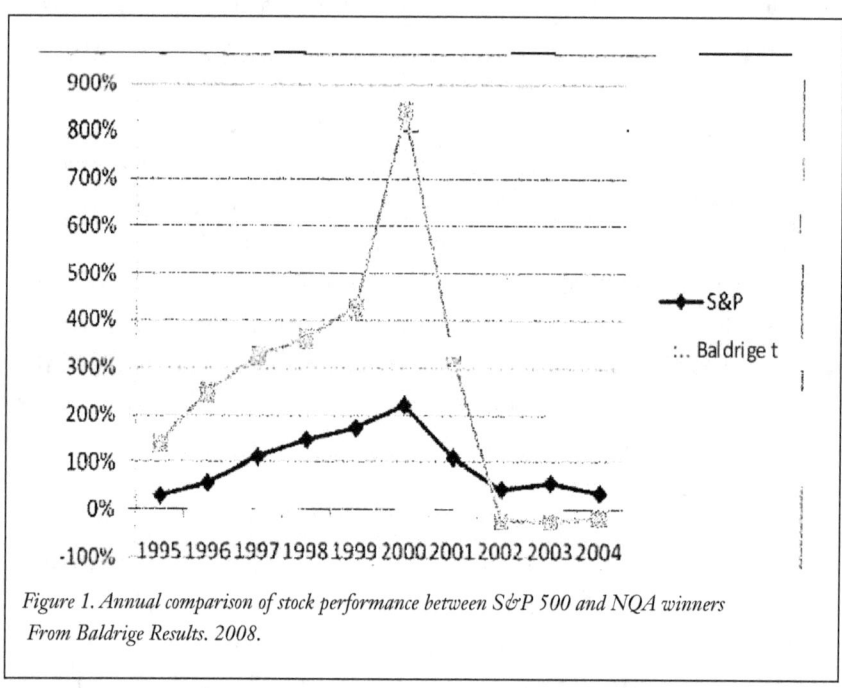

Figure 1. Annual comparison of stock performance between S&P 500 and NQA winners From Baldrige Results. 2008.

Foma (2012) linked MBNQA criteria with the internal assessment of operations and found that such a relationship allows higher productivity and improved employee relations. Also, organizations were able to increase market share and gain higher customer satisfaction, resulting in improved profitability. The greatest benefit is the increase in furthering improvements across the organization. With all the information and research considered, the adoption and implementation of the MBNQA criteria for performance excellence can be an effective tool when fully implemented in an organization. According to Beard and Humphrey (2014), earning the MBNQA is not a roadmap for success; however, sustaining improvements and refining more processes in order to Improve continually are considered long-term keys to success.

Dilemmas and Criticism

Organizations must meet the predefined performance criteria in order to earn the MBNQA. The multidimensional criteria for the award are based on various fundamental, organizational attributes. Companies have to make significant changes in order to qualify. Management cannot always completely adopt the performance management model of an award winning company. A major dilemma that a majority of the organizations face as they seek to attain the MBNQA occurs when management do not adequately audit the internal organizational analysis and fail to decipher the TQM requirements of the company. The internal analysis provides the managers with a strategic direction and performance issues that have to be bolstered. Another dilemma caused by a lack of inadequate internal organizational analysis is that the management prior to the implementation of the TQM initiative becomes dependent on the adopted benchmark model (Griffith et al., 2012).

However, from the beginning, there have been arguments about the financial importance of winning the award. One reason for questioning the merits of the MBNQA is the accuracy of the judging process. Companies such as Cadillac, Motorola, Federal Express, and Wallace Company have never won any top ratings in quality or customer satisfaction survey even though it could be argued that these companies have at one time maintained higher quality and competitiveness over their competitors.

Second, finances are supposed to be a factor, but many of these companies fall short of performance excellence. For instance, the Wallace Company of Houston, Texas, faced bankruptcy one-year after winning the MBNQA. Additionally, many feel that the award can be essentially bought by large companies because there is no limit to how many applications a company can submit. For example, Xerox in 1987 and Corning in 1989, both spent over $800,000 and 14,000 hours in preparing applications for submission. Smaller firms may not have the resources needed to compete for the award in this way. Furthermore, many more hours and resources were spent coaching employees for the site evaluations required by Baldrige examiners (Jacob et al., 2004; Verhoef & Leeflang, 2009). It is evident from these examples that financial importance of winning the award is increasingly being called into question.

Since the MBNQA is considered the highest award for quality in the U.S., this researcher believes it not only gives praise to the deserving companies, but also provides a goal so every company can strive through its effort of improving its services and products. While criticism points out that some companies are stronger in some areas, they fail to see the overall picture and make their assumptions without all of the facts.

According to Foma (2012), only 15 companies out of millions in the U.S., applied for the award because they thought the award was solely for manufacturers, when that is not the case.

Jacob et al. (2012) reported that although the awardees are very successful in particular instances, they are not convincing that the techniques for quality management in a limited number of organizations can improve the quality of services and products in entire institutions. Another major criticism of the MBNQA, as indicated by Jacob et al. (2004) and Verhoef and Leeflang (2009), is the framework is not based on any empirical evidence and limited research has been done on the issue given the requirements of data confidentiality of public as well as private sector organizations. Wilson et al. (2003) reported that even NIST, which oversees the award and is the only source of complete data, has its own requirements for confidentiality and it does not allow using the aggregate data for the purpose of scrutiny. There are valid reasons for NIST's refusal, but without the data, a serious study of quality principles will continue to be hampered. Another argument against the award is that it does not provide any higher roadmap of performance, although it provides a framework for value-based leadership and employee engagement (Griffith et al., 2012). Therefore, due to the non-prescriptive nature of MBNQA, it is not possible to determine actions that are right for achieving overall objectives of the criteria. Based on assumption, some of the organizations that embark on the Malcolm Baldrige Criteria for Performance Excellence would like to win the MBNQA, whereas others are merely striving to improve overall quality within their organization.

Focusing mainly on the award has negative side effects as it results in stress among the employees when filling out and submitting the application (Peng & Prybutok, 2014). This means that it can be dangerous to emphasize making process improvements solely for the purpose of competing for the award at the expense of making sound business decisions. One such examples comes from the survey conducted in 1996, reporting that of approximately one million copies of the criteria that had been distributed since 1987, about 180,000 were thrown away and 891,000 were used at least once.

Additionally, the survey showed that of the 819,000, 70.7% were used as a source of a framework for process improvement and only 23.69% were used to apply for the MBNQA (Bailey, 2011).

Duarte et al. (2013) and Griffith et al. (2012) explained the way in which MBNQA is broadly recognized in the leaders' groups from the sector of education, manufacturing, healthcare, and small businesses, where all organizations were Fortune 100 companies. The results of the survey showed that more than 70% of the leaders of these organizations did not have any in-depth knowledge of the criteria and the implementation requirements, although they agreed on using the criteria in the future.

Cazzell and Ulmer (2009) sought to explain adoption problems regarding the criteria and found that the major issues were lack of familiarity, perceived or real complexity of the criteria, lack of understanding the components, and the costs associated in implementing were the same. Berber, Pasula, and Radosevic (2012) included another barrier to be the related logistics and resource requirements of applying for the MBNQA. Also, the role of leadership remained crucial in the implementation process of the Baldrige Criteria (Wilson & Collier, 2000). It is critical to address the emerging organizational changes in a positive manner for accompanying the adoption and implementation of the Baldrige Criteria. The website of awards related to the financial excellence of the winners of the award is compared to the performance of non-winners.

Lee et al. (2014) reported that the small sample size can be misleading and distortive as the results are skewed by fewer performers, resulting in the excellent performance of all MBNQA winners, which is not always the case.

Jacob et al. (2012) argued that the MBNQA winners do not appear to yield better financial results than other companies. The researchers reviewed all MBNQA winners from 1988 to 1999 and found that the winners did outperform the market, but that it was possible to have a portfolio of competing firms that outperformed MBNQA winners.

Another area of weakness for the MBNQA was the winners of the award have a weak system of information, unclear definitions of quality, lack of alignment, partially adopted system of quality management, lack of measures, failures to use listening posts, and passive indicators (Cazzell & Ulmer, 2009; Choi et al., 2009; Mena & Hult, 2009). Also, the costs of applying the MBNQA were high, along with increased investments in hours of labor for purpose of documentation and application preparation. There were also costs attached in making the workforce ready to visit the site.

Beyond the aforementioned weaknesses pointed out in the MBNQA criteria and implementation, Curkovic et a1. (2000) acknowledged the lack of research in the Baldrige process with improved financial performances based on the evidence that the criteria were vague and not clearly interpretable. Also, the commitment of top management to total quality improvement posed a limiting factor for the award given the lack of correlation between the profit potential and market competitiveness for the award recipient (Galvin, 1991; Griffith et a1., 2012). There are cases when the award has not brought an expected increase in sales and growth in earnings, but has resulted in only wastage of the organization's resources and time. Griffith et al. (2012) also showed the possibility that the examination team does not understand the criteria or assessment process well enough.

Besides the issues related to commitment and resources, the MBNQA has been found to focus on the processes, meaning that the award fails to measure the actual service or product that the organization offers to the customers (Lee et a1., 2014).

According to, organizations opting for the award might lose ground for the quality program implementation after the initial improvement. The failure rate for quality improvement initiatives remains 15% to 50% (Hossain & Prybutok, 2014).

Quality Management and Firm's Performance
Product quality is a key factor in any decision because it makes it easier for the customer to choose the right product. Normally, the buyer requests samples from potential suppliers and then the process of inspection and

examination takes place. In some situations, buyers are forced to send technical experts to assess quality management systems. In order to reduce the problems caused by actual nature and high cost, buyers have been forced to assess the quality system for better resources. The need has emerged to make sure quality has universal criteria for any product or service. Companies must have a comprehensive quality system to satisfy the needs of internal management. It is also necessary for the purpose of contracting and quality assessment to demonstrate the implementation of the elements. Following are the definitions of quality as presented by the ISO:

1. Overall quality characteristics of a substance determine its ability to meet the needs described or contained.
2. Quality policy is defined as the desire and direction of an organization in terms of quality as set by senior management.
3. Quality management is defined as the activities of the overall management function that determines policy of quality, objectives, and responsibilities. It has implementation through such means such as quality planning, quality control, QA, and quality improvement within quality requirements.
4. Quality control is defined as the operational technique and activity used to meet the quality requirements.
5. All QA activities get plotted and carried out within the organization. It describes the need to secure or is confident enough to find someone who could meet quality requirements.
6. It identifies the episode that affects the quality of the product, such as inspection, marketing, service, product development, manufacturing engineering, and purchase of production (Adam, 1994).

Quality Standard

A document issued as a result of consensus that sets forth the requirements which must be determined by the product, process, or service is quality standard. At the company level, the main objective of standardization is to increase the company's profitability. At the international level, its overriding objective is to promote trade between countries and to remove the technical obstacles that occur in various sectors.

The standard product requirements are determined to make it the best material. The scale instrument even determines the product specifications or standards that must be provided in the product, tailored to the requirements of the customer. It authorizes the fundamental principle in the certification of the product, such as the licensing to use a product. It gets confirmation so the product is compatible with requirements. It faces approval and gets ratified according to the product specifications of the donor recognized like certificate. It even requires periodic monitoring of the company's products attached to the certificate (Brooks, 2005).

It includes the quality system of organization structure, procedures, processes, and resources needed to implement a comprehensive quality management system in order to achieve quality objectives. It is identified as a measure of the quality system to ensure quality management in the company in order to make sure the products are compatible with the standards set by the organization. The company is free to develop any level of quality for its products on the basis of considerations for marketing and customer requirements. It also helps to gauge the quality system to achieve the desired level of quality. In the case of contracting, it assists in implementing a system, such as ISO 9000. The company then understands the customer requirements and manages different functional departments in a manner to ensure the final product and service meet all requirements of the contract (ISO, 2008).

Conclusion

Given this discussion on the significance as well as weaknesses of the MBNQA criteria, it remains important to assess the financial performance of the awarded organizations based on the impact of winning the MBQNA. For this purpose, the factors of leadership, internal assessment, commitment to quality initiatives, and the validity of criteria needs to be incorporated in the financial performance measurement of the organization. The next chapter discusses the methodology for the proposed study, explaining the research design, strategy, philosophy, and methods, along with the sample size and methods of data collection and analysis.

CHAPTER THREE: METHODOLOGY

This study used financial metrics to show changes in the performance of firms that have won the MBNQA. It compared the firms' performance five years before and five years after winning the MBNQA and compares their performance with key competitors. The difference between this study and previous studies is that it focused on internal measures of performance instead of the external measure of the stock price.

This chapter introduced the research and data analysis techniques used. The study was quantitative and relied on secondary data to provide substantive evidence on events regarding the performance of the companies under study. Appropriate analysis techniques were chosen to facilitate a comparison between those firms that won the MBNQA and key competitors. The analysis includes pictorial display of the data, descriptive statistical measures, and some inferential statistical tools.

The design for this quantitative study seeks to determine if winning the MBQNA (IV)results in better firm performance (DV). The purpose of the award leads the researcher to believe that the winning company is the best in the ROE, MVA, EVA, and ROA (i.e., firm performance). Although some companies may outperform MBNQA winning companies in some areas, winning companies outperform their competitors in many other areas, making them the overall winners. However, some factors seem to be deemed more important than others.

Purpose Statement

The purpose of this research is to examine if winning the MBQNA (IV) has a significant effect on firm performance, as measured by ROA (DV). The list of MBNQA winners in an 11-year period (2004-2015) formed the basis of this study.

Research Question

This study examined the following research questions:
- Does winning the Malcolm Baldrige National Quality Award (MBNQA) result in an improved Return on Assets (ROA)?
- Has winning the MBNQA been an effective tool for advancing organizations, as it indicates is the intent of the award?

To answer this question, this study did the following:
1. Examined the impact of winning the MBQNA in firm performance as measured by ROA.
2. Examined the relationship between MBNQA and ROA.

Hypotheses

A multiple regression was used to determine the effect winning the MBNQA and other variables has on the identified DV (ROA). The following statistical hypotheses was be tested:

Hal: BROE #0 where BRoE is the slope of whether the firm has won the MBNQA. That is, winning the MBNQA has a statistically significant effect on ROA.

Ha2: BROA # 0, where BRoA is the slope of other individual IVs (to be identified by this study). That is, each specific variable has a statistically significant effect on the ROA. These hypotheses are essential to understanding the winning firm's performance in context of the prevailing market conditions at the time of the study. A challenge in determining shareholder valuation is to differentiate the performance of a firm from the rising tide- phenomenon. That is, a firm that performs well when all of its competitors perform equally well is not increasing shareholder value at an exceptional rate, only a normal rate. A more direct signal of exceptional shareholder value creation is a firm that increases its value while its key competitors do not perform well. The efficient market hypothesis (EMH) indicates that the market generated signals equally to investors and, in time, investors reacted in an appropriate manner.

Research Methodology

The current research intends to follow a quantitative, non-experimental correlational research design to examine if winning the MBQNA (IV) results in better ROA (DV). This quantitative study used a multiple regression to determine if there is a correlation between earning the MBQNA and ROA. This research project focused on MBNQA winning companies that may not have earned the award through their quality or market returns. Other DVs include ROE, MVA, and EVA (i.e., firm performance).

ROA is measured in terms of net income divided by total assets and had its entire focus on how a firm is profitable relative to its total assets. Similarly, ROE measured in terms of net income to shareholder's equity, indicating the amount of net income that is being received out of total investment provided by shareholders in the firm. While it may first appear as though it is impossible to utilize a quantitative approach to this particular research question, due to a lack of a common measure of achievement present in organizational results as a result of the wide range of organizations that have applied for and summarily won MBNQAs, all that is needed is a common measure of achievement of a given organization's results. This measure may be implied regarding the following statement relating to the award:

The 99 Baldrige Award winners (including 6 two-time winners) serve as national role models for U.S. organizations. For these two-time role models, median growth in number of sites between awards was 84%, median growth in revenue was 92.5%, and median growth in jobs was 65.5%. By comparison, according to statistics from the Bureau of Economic Analysis and the Bureau of Labor Statistics, average growth in jobs was 2.5% for a matched set of industries and time periods for each recipient.

This indicates that a commonality may be found across all organizations, regardless of performance industry, in terms of the overall growth of the organization in comparison to other organizations, indicating that the winner of the award has advanced more than other organizations in its industry in at least one way. There are many different ways to determine the advancement of the organization, including the organization's overall ROA, which allows for the identification of the percentage of profits earned by an organization in relation to the overall resources available to the organization.

EVA is the variable that measures the financial performance of an organization based on the calculated residual wealth (Priester & Wang, 2010). Stem (1993), Stewart (1991), and Priester and Wang (2010) suggested that the EVA indicator has been used in the accounting literature extensively. The concept of EVA originated in the microeconomic literature and has been used to try and establish a link between a firm's earnings and shareholders' wealth creation. It is an indicator used to measure economic profit. EVA is the result of subtracting the opportunity cost of invested capital from the net operating profit after tax. The opportunity cost can be determined by multiplying the weighted average cost of debt and equity capital by the amount of capital employed.

Stem and Stewart argued that unlike some other performance indicators such as earnings per share (EPS) or earnings before interest, taxes, depreciation, and amortization (EBITDA), EVA gauges both operating and financial activities. Stem (1993) and Stewart (1991) suggested that companies that apply EVA in their performance measurement can use several methods to increase this indicator and their performance (Priester & Wang, 2010), including:

- Improving the net operating profit after tax generated by existing capital.
- Reducing the debt or equity capital employed.
- Investing in potential projects where the return on investment (ROI) of this investment exceeds the weighted average cost of capital.
- Divesting capital where the ROI of the project is less than the weighted average cost of capital.

In a comparative study, Haddad (2012) contrasted intellectual capital with EVA. For example, in terms of financial representation, he argued that EVA ties financial calculation and risk with investment indicators. However, the financial and non-financial indicators are loosely tied with Invested Capital (IC) from an IC perspective. With respect to growth, future growth is based on capital and cost structures of the firm from an EVA perspective. However, future growth is a representation of human, organizational, and relational capital development from an IC perspective. For EVA, strategies are determined based on the net present value calculation. For IC, strategies are determined based on the need to increase productivity and creativity. Therefore, the objectives for the two measurement methods are different. Brigham and Ehrhardt

(2013) argued, although the EVA method was not developed to measure the value of intangible assets, several intellectual capital studies have discussed it when reviewing the methods to measure IC.

Although the previous literature suggested EVA might be used as an indicator to measure the flow of IC, Brigham and Ehrhardt (2013) questioned the appropriateness of this indicator in measuring the value added of intangible resources. As evidenced by Stem (1993) and Stewart (1991), the suggested indicators might outperform some traditional financial performance in measuring wealth. However, it does not separate wealth creation into tangible and intangible sources.

In the quest for creating value, multinational companies such as General Electric, Coca Cola, Siemens, Sony, and AT&T have already used EVA as a performance measurement tool for management system (Ray, 2010, p. 117). Tong et al. (2010) stated "build a performance evaluation system based on Economic Value Added and Balanced Scorecard for logistics enterprises empirically and found that EVA gets significantly positive Kendall's correlation with strategic objective whose proxy is corporate value" (p. 122). Wang and Fan (2010) said "a performance model based on EVA method that focus on value creation attending comprehensive measurement of service oriented enterprises. The result showed that service center of issuing has a negative EVA although its profit is positive" (p. 122).

MVA shows the difference between the market value of a company and the capital contributed by investors (both bondholders and shareholders). In other words, it is the sum of all capital claims held against the company, plus the market value of debt and equity (Wang & Fan, 2010).

Justification for the Methodology and Statistical Analysis

The appropriateness of the quantitative method for the current study stems from the study's goal of collecting objective, numeric data for testing associations among variables by using statistical methods (Dyer, 2006). The quantitative method is particularly useful for answering research questions related to measurement of variables, testing of theories, and prediction of outcomes (Dyer, 2006; Neuman, 2003). The quantitative method was chosen because the data investigated were quantified in nature, as opposed to the use of more subjective, qualitative data. In addition, the lack of an experimental design indicates the need to utilize already published literature from primary and secondary sources of a fiscal nature, which places the study exclusively in the quantitative realm.

Similarly, the appropriateness of the correlational design for the current study derives from the study's goal to test associations among IV (MBQNA) and a DV (ROA). The literature has shown that a correlational design is the most appropriate quantitative approach for examining associations among variables, without inferring causality (Sproull, 2002; Tabachnick & Fidell, 2001a, 2001b).

Study Population and Data Collection

The population under examination were the NQA firms and a random selection of key competitors in similar industries from 2004-2015. In order to see how winning the MBNQA added value to the recipients, the researcher intends to collect data from Yahoo finance articles, publicly traded articles, NIST, and other sources, using search words such as antecedents to superior firm performance. The target population of the study was 100 companies that have won the MBNQA. It is impossible to target all the companies that have won the MBNQA. The participants in the instrument were selected using random sampling. In this type of sampling technique, each of the population elements has an equal chance of being selected in the sample (Fowler, 2009).

Data was collected using secondary source data and entered into SPSST ^ (Statistical Package for the Social Sciences) software for analysis using a multivariate regression. In performing the study, the research material was collected from the Internet, publically traded journals, ProQuest, EBSCOhost, and peer reviewed journals as sources of information. This study used an 11-year period of data collection (2004-2015) and a sample of 100 companies that have received the award. Secondary data were gathered to help uncover valuable information that is impossible to gain in limited research. Secondary research was used to provide the latest theoretical and academic information about the 100 companies investigated and yield evidence to support the research obtained from graphs, tables, or opinions made based on previously collected data, enabling the writer to understand and analyze what others have written on the subject (National Institute of Standards and Technology, 2011).

Analysis Tool

The analysis was carried out in accordance with the response of the secondary data gathered from previous studies and analyzed using SPSS. The next step was to put the data into SPSS, perform statistical analysis, interpret the data, and make recommendations.

The IV ran a linear regression against specific DVs resulting in a correlation (Pearson's R) that indicated the overall strength of association between the IV and DVs. The Coefficient of Determination (R-squared), indicating the proportion of variation in the DVs explained by the IVs, and slope (or coefficient B), depicts the actual effect each IV has on the DV. A comparison of the slopes with adjusted R-squared indicated which IVs have the greatest effect and to what extent.

Validity and Reliability

As the data for this study was raw data from recognized and established data collection institutions such as the Bureau of Labor Statistics, NIST, publically traded 'journals, and other sources, no data collection instrument was used or designed for this specific study. The validity of the data was assumed to be robust.

Several statistical tests were conducted, and the quantitative method is used. The population examined is firm tracked both five years before and five years after the NQA competition and award. Secondly, the firm performance of the winning firms were compared with their key competitors. The research assumption was that by winning a NQA, a firm becomes more efficient and effective in the marketplace.

The literature review revealed that the strategic management process has evolved to advanced levels of complexity Health (1988, 2010) and Neely, Gregory, and Platts (2005) referred "to the performance measurement systems (PMS) as the set of metrics used to quantify both efficiency and effectiveness" (p. 3). Furthermore, the literature defined "measures as metrics used to quantify and compute an action's efficiency and effectiveness" (Bourne & Neely, 2003, p. 3; Hubbard, Parsons, Nelson, & Carey, 2009).

As a consequence, knowledge of the actual operationalization of the strategy process remains sparse. Focusing on firm performance and selecting the winners of the MBNQA, the present research identified the key aspects of the strategic process and the associated data-driven measures. It illustrated the key performance metrics used by decision makers who lead organizations in the strategy process. The findings helped narrow the gap in prior studies.

Conceptual Mode

The conceptual framework of this study is developed from an examination of current performance analysis practices. While many financial practitioners advocate using stock price to establish shareholder valuations, the underlying assumption is that the (EMH) is valid. The central question of this study is whether winning a NQA helps the firm or not. Attempts to verify this correlation using stock price have not been conclusive. Fama (1995) indicated that stock prices are random in nature and would eventually reflect the true value of a firm. Stock price is one of the numerous measures of firm performance. For example, ROI and EVA are equally important to ensure corporate governance, especially with respect to the Sarbanes-Oxley Act of 2002 (Epstein & Hanson, 2005).

Theoretical Model

The goal of this study was to compare the measures of output in business performance in relation to measures of inputs used to derive those outputs. In this case, shareholder value by way of profits. Harrison (1994) used an open systems model to diagnose organizations. "Performance is a recurrent theme, widely and loosely used in all fields of management. Although it has become the mantra of recent years in almost all organizations, a clear and explicit definition is still missing" (Franco-Santos et al., 2007). This model was a representation of value-adding activities' performance in order to create a product or service. It starts with inputs that are all types of labor and non- labor resources owned by the organization. Internal procedures converts these resource inputs into a finished product or service. However, these internal processes are supported by four other factors to support production: (a) technology, (b) goals and strategy, (c) culture, and (d) structure. As comprehensive as this process is, it is not set in isolation, but is contained within a contextual environment external to the organization.

This study aligns the logic of the open systems model with Generally Accepted Accounting Principles (GAAP) and associated financial reporting requirements of the U.S. Securities and Exchange Commission.

Definition of Variables

The goal of this study is to determine if there is evidence that an organization is more efficient following its preparation for and its subsequent winning of a NQA using accounting data to indicate efficiency. Efficiency in this context refers to the measures of effective production relative to the expenditure of resources ("Efficiency," n.d.). In the context of this study, efficiency is the productivity of using company assets as represented on the balance sheet, with the sales and income performance as shown on the income statement. The measures of production in this study represent assets (resources). Those factors converts into profit. The results of the consumption of the factors occurred because of that consumption. The reason for the selection of these data points is that they are all essential parts of a company's annual 10-K filing that represents the company's final audited financial report of operations for the year. This is required by the U.S. Securities and Exchange Commission ("Form 10-K," 2006). These variables also represent key indicators from both the balance sheet and income statement.

The following are the dependent variables for this study:

1. Returns on assets (ROA). This is a measure of how effectively a firm converts assets, which appear on the balance sheet, to income. It is calculate by dividing the net income by assets. ROA is "a basic measure of the efficiency with which a company allocates and manages its resources" (Higgins, 2007, p. 39). The rationale for selecting this variable is that it integrates a key metric from the balance sheet (i.e., assets) with a key metric from the income statement (i.e., net income). The testing of ROA in this study extends the work of Heras, Casadesus, and Dick (2002) and Martinez-Costa and Martinez-Lorente (2007). Both of these studies used r-tests in a similar manner in this study. That is, they used r-tests to analyze company ROA before and after firms were awarded

41

ISO 9000 certification, a process similar in nature to the NQA evaluation process. The goal of their studies was to establish evidence for shareholder value of quality initiatives. A final justification for using ROA is that it enables cross-sectional and inter-temporal comparisons of firm performance (Healy, Palepu, & Ruback, 1992). This enables the comparisons, for instance, of large firms and small firms because the metric does not use an absolute value, such as sales, but instead is the ratio of two performance metrics.

2. Earnings per Share (EPS). The rationale for selecting this factor was that "EPS of common stock is a way to measure profitability from the point of view of the common shareholder" (Vance, 2003, p. 34). The EPS tells the shareholders, "How much earning power and how much dividend income you would be getting for each share you buy?" (Williams, Haka, Bettner, & Carcello, 2006, p. 560). In this way, EPS serves as a key measure of shareholder valuation. It is important enough, in fact, that "often it is the basis for setting specific corporate objectives and goals as part of strategic planning" (Helfert, 2003, p. 132). There are two kinds of EPS, basic and diluted. The number of shares of common stock provides the basis for calculating the undiluted EPS. Many firms issue preferred stOck, however, which can be converted to common stock, and "the conversion of this preferred stock would increase the number of common share outstanding and might dilute (reduce) earnings per share" (Williams et al., 2006, p. 563). While the conversion is not always done, the diluted EPS tells the shareholders what could have happened to their EPS had the conversion been done (Williams et al., 2006). With this fact in mind, the diluted EPS value is used for all EPS calculations.

3. Another consideration in using EPS is whether or not to include extraordinary items in the calculation. Extraordinary items are "transactions and events that are unusual in nature and occur infrequently" (Williams et al., 2006, p. 577). For purposes of this study, extraordinary items were included in the EPS calculations. The use of ROA and EPS follows the work of who sought to establish the value to shareholders of ISO 9000 certification (Chow-Cua, Goh, & Wan, 2003). These variables, ROA, and EPS are also among the financial performance indicators for

strategic business performance as noted by Beattie and Sohal (1999). Consequently, they are of high importance to shareholders for both near-term and long-term considerations.

4. Current ratio. The current ratio is a measure of a firm's liquidity. It is calculated by dividing the current assets by the current liabilities. The rationale for selecting this variable for analysis is that the current ratio is important from the investor's viewpoint as it indicates the firm's ability to manage on operating income and not rely on outside financing (Higgins, 2007). This variable was chosen to act as a counterbalance to ROA. That is, this metric provides shareholders with information to ensure that a firm does not incur increased risks to its financial

liquidity by undermining its current ratio in its quest to increase ROA. Morin and Jarrell (2001) indicated this concern as well when they stated, "value can be created for equity holders by increasing financial leverage (debt) up to a point" (p. 414). The current ratio then acts as a measure of the risk a company incurs in balancing its asset base with its liabilities. In fact, this component is so important to financial performance that often the overstatement of assets and/or the understatement of liabilities are found in financial fraud cases. Mulford and Comiskey (2002) stated, "An overstatement of assets or understatement of liabilities can be directly linked to an increase in earnings. As earnings are increased, so are retained earnings, leading to a direct increment to shareholders' equity" (p. 239).

Data Collection

Sample

Sampling techniques was not used in this study, as the entire population of NQA winners were examined. As the entire population of NQA is small to begin with, there was no need to use sampling techniques, nor would there have been any of the stated advantages of performing sampling, such as decreased cost, reduced time, or increased accuracy (Sanders & Smidt, 2000).

The sample in this study consisted of MBNQA winning organizations. At the time of this study, there were 86 award winning organizations that had received 91 awards since the inception of the MBNQA program in the sectors of manufacturing, small business, service, education, healthcare, and non-profit. Table 1 depicts the MBNQA recipients by category since inception.

Table 1

MBNQA Recipients by Category from 1988 to 2010

Manufacturing	Small Business	Service	Healthcare	Education	Non-profit	Total
30	22	15	12	9	3	91

In 1999, the NIST first published the award application documents, which are accessible on the NIST website. By the end of 2010, 56 awards had been granted to 54 organizations. Table 2 depicts the MBNQA recipients by category from 1999 to the end of 2010.

Table 2

MBNQA Recipients by Category from 1999 to 2010

Manufacturing	Small Business	Service	Healthcare	Education	Non-profit	Total
12	13	7	12	9	3	56

The sampling frame of this quantitative study was composed of 32 MBNQA recipients in the sectors of manufacturing, small business, and service. Employing theory-based sampling, a purposive sample was defined based on conceptual considerations (Eisenhardt, 1989; Eisenhardt & Graebner, 2007). In this case, there is likelihood those cases would enable the researcher to gain insights into the applied strategic management process. Given its focus on the operationalization of the strategic process in the business setting, this study investigated the application documents of MBNQA recipients in manufacturing, small business, and service from 1999 to 2010. Table 3 depicts the-sample of 32 MBNQA recipients by category. Target Population

Table 3

MBNQA Recipients Sample from 1999 to 2010

Manufacturing	Small Business	Service	Total
12	13	7	32

The population under examination is a set of firms whose performance was tracked both five years before and five years after the NQA competition and award. The desired outcome of this research was to develop a theory. The study employed theoretical sampling, as this allows case selection based on the suitability of cases for illuminating and extending relationships and logic among constructs (Eisenhardt, 1989; Eisenhardt & Graebner, 2007). This study did not use a probability sample. Cases were selected based on the likelihood they would lead to insights into the strategic management process practiced by a group of companies (Glaser & Strauss, 1971). In other words, the cases were selected based on their propensity to provide insights, replicate findings from other cases, be contrasted to other cases, eliminate alternative explanations, or elaborate on the emergent theory (Eisenhardt & Graebner, 2007). The result was a purposive sample that accentuated the action plans, procedures, measures, and strategic objectives and goals of senior decision-makers in the strategic management process (Kuzel, 1992; Morse, 1989; Eisenhardt & Graebner, 2007).

Inclusion Criteria

The results of this study are designed to measure how the winner of the award has advanced following the receipt of the award. A common measure of performance could be generated for the inclusion of non-profit and for-profit firms, given the fact that in 2010 the MBNQA was changed to the Baldrige Performance Excellence Program as it was believed that this name served to better reflect an evolution toward a focus on quality, regardless if the quality was of a product, service, or customer quality with a strategic focus on overall organizational quality. Due to the time limitations of this particular research study, only those firms satisfying both the criteria given as follows were included in the study:

1. Firms operating in a business environment. Firms in manufacturing, firms in educations or health services categories were not included for the study.
2. Firms that are publically traded. Privately held firms were not used as this study requires credible, high-quality financial performance for study variables.

The nominees came from all sectors, including six in the service category, three in manufacturing, four in health care, three in higher education, and one each in the non- profit and government categories (Gottlieb, 2015).

Table 4

MBNQA Recipients by Category from 2010 to 2015

Manufacturing	Small Business	Service	Healthcare	Education	Non-profit	Total
30	22	15	12	9	10	100

The 2014 Baldrige Award recipients, listed with their category, are:
- PricewaterhouseCoopers Public Sector Practice, McLean, Virginia (service)
- Hill Country Memorial, Fredericksburg, Texas (health care)
- St. David's HealthCare, Austin, Texas (health care)
- Elevations Credit Union, Boulder, Colorado (nonprofit)

The 2015 Baldrige Award recipients, listed with their category, are:
- Lockheed Martin Missiles and Fire Control, Grand Prairie, TX (manufacturing)
- MESA Products Inc., Tulsa, OK (small business)
- North Mississippi Health Services, Tupelo, MS (health care)
- City of Irving, Irving, Texas (nonprofit)

Steps for NQA Winners

Data Collection Process for NQA Winners

A multi-stepped process was used for choosing the NQA winners. First, the MBNQA website was examined to identify the winners for all years from the inception of the program in 1988 ("1988-2007 Award Recipients' Contacts and Profiles," 2008).

- From the list of all winners, those that were in the education or health services categories were eliminated, as the focus of this study is performance in a business environment and not the education or health services fields.

- Next, only those firms that are publicly traded were considered because of the need for published financial performance data. Credible financial data on publicly traded firms is available on numerous commercial databases such as Value Line Datafile. The U.S. Security and Exchange Commission's Electronic Data Gathering, Analysis, and Retrieval (EDGAR) database also used to gather financial data on publicly traded U.S. business ("SEC Filings & Forms [EDG1." n.d.) only those firms that had sufficient number of years of data available both before and after the year of their NQA award-date were considered.

- The quarterly 10-Q reports provide 20 data points for each of the three variables for each of the NQA-winning firms under study. This established a baseline of 10 quarterly data points before and during the first half of the award year, and 10 data points during the latter part of the award year and after, in order to address research question. This interval gives a sufficient time to moderate seasonal variations and is considered a long-term horizon and not short or medium term (Groebner, Shannon, Fry, & Smith, 2005). In this manner, a five-year period was deemed sufficiently long to compare business performance before and after the NQA award date. Research question, however, is only concerned with testing the NQA-winning firm with its competitors, from year of award through five years (business cycles) thereafter. This is a total of 10 quarterly data points for the three variables.

Instrumentation

The instrumentation plan consists of several decisions, including how to gather the data, when to gather data, where to gather data, and how to analyze results (Blankenship, 2009). The research method aids in identifying the type of data to be gathered; in this case, a quantitative study was selected. The data regarding the winning companies has been collected from the NIST website and contained in a simple and easy to understand format in Microsoft Excel. The financial data of the companies was the next information to be collected, gathered from various financial websites as indicated above, and entered manually into the spreadsheet itself. Data has already been made available for these companies both prior to their receipt of the award and following the receipt of the award. Results were analyzed from this Excel document in order to allow for the proving or disproving of the hypotheses and the addressing of the identified research questions.

Procedures

The instrumentation covers the plan or course of action to be used by the researcher for the purpose of completing a given research study, while the instrument is the device that is used for the completion of the study (Biddix, 2014). The data gathering procedures, data analysis procedures, and the limitations and delimitations of the study are contained within this section (Roberts, 2010).

Data Gathering

Data were collected through the use of secondary sources associated with the identification and representation of data. As there were no human participants in the research study, there was no need for the design of instructions or the gathering of informed consent. Data were collected from various financial websites regarding company projections and was obtained from NIST directly regarding the specific list of MBNQA winners.

Data Analysis

As this study uses a quantitative, non-experimental, correlational research design, a multiple regression analysis was completed via Excel in order to analyze the data.

Valuations for each of the different companies regarding their performance for the ten- year span were entered into Excel and a correlational analysis was completed for the purpose of identifying whether or not there was any relation between firm performance and the winning of the MBNQA. The results were then reviewed and written up for discussion in Chapter Five of the dissertation.

Limitations

There are several limitations present within the study itself. These include the limited ability to compare MBQNA winners in all industries, the limited financial data available on certain organizations, and there are still different industries being utilized in the comparison. In addition, there is an inability to control industry associated factors or economic factors, such as the concern regarding the use of financial data recorded for organizations during the recession of the early 2000s, an economic consideration that can result in potentially skewed data due to the fact that the correlational analysis looks only at the data input and does not take into account dips in a particular industry or overall country economy. For example, a low correlation may be received, but if the recession could be taken into account effectively, there may be a positive correlation based on the data for a given industry as a whole during that time and the firm's comparison to its competitors during that same period of time.

Delimitations

The delimitations of a given study work to limit the influences that constrict the overall capacities of the study (Creswell, 2013). As such, the delimitations identified for the completion of the study were the reduction of the sample size to organizations who won the MBNQA, whose data was published within the set timeframe identified, who were only in certain industries, and whose financial records for five years prior and five years after were available.

Key Competitors of NQA Winners

The statistical approach used in this study is to measure the performance of certain firms/organizations variables and compare it to a comparable portfolio of firms to see if evidence existed of a difference in performance between the two. The rationale for making this comparison is twofold. First, it is to externally validate the NQA-winning firms against the market segment as a whole. A risk of excluding these external validation points is that an NQA-winning firm's performance may have increased after winning, but, the improvement may have been due to an overall improvement in the market sector. The second reason is to mitigate the effects of non-obvious factors that influenced the performance outcomes. Factors that were not included in this study.

The method of selecting the key competitors involved first identifying the primary Standard Industrial Classification (SIC) classification codes of the NQA winners as shown in the EDGAR record. The SIC codes represent the classification of the kind business performed by companies. The total market sales within the SIC were then calculated to determine the significant and non-significant competitors. The percentage of total sales for all listed firms was sorted in descending order, with the company with the highest market share heading the list. For the purposes of this study, the key competitors were those companies whose market share exceeded 3% of the total sales of the SIC and collectively constituted a majority of the market. This eliminated many non-significant competitors whose market share was sometimes a fraction of 1%. Market share data are shown in Chapter Four.

Performance Excellence Program (BPEP)

This study collected publicly available existing secondary data from the Baldrige Performance Excellence Program (BPEP), which shares the documents of MBNQA winning organizations with the public. The goal of the BPEP is to foster U.S. innovation and industrial competitiveness by advancing measurement science, standards, and technology through an active public-private partnership (NIST, 2011). The partnership seeks to improve cooperation between the private sector and all levels of government to advance national competitiveness. BPEP is subdivided into various organizations and functions, each serving a defined purpose and playing an important role in the program's continued growth and success. NIST is responsible for managing and promoting BPEP.

The American Society for Quality (ASQ) assists in the administration of the program. The Board of Overseers provides advice and assesses all aspects of the program with the intent of ensuring the adequacy of the criteria and the applied processes for determining award recipients (Calhoun, 2002). Most importantly, it is responsible for evaluating the program's capacity to promote performance excellence among U.S. based organizations. Finally, the Board of Examiners assesses the performance excellence of applicant organizations. It is made up of experts from U.S. organizations that have taken an Examiner Preparation Course. The Board of Examiners is also responsible for the evaluation of award applications and provides feedback reports to the participating organizations (National Institute of Standards and Technology, 2011).

The award applications document the various companies' commitment to improved competitiveness and are used to advance performance excellence across U.S. organizations by making information on successful performance strategies publicly available. The information fits the Baldrige Criteria for Performance Excellence Framework (CPEF), a non-prescriptive conceptual blueprint of a results-oriented exemplar management system centered on beliefs and behaviors (National Institute of Standards and Technology, 2011). This study focused on seven components of the MBNQA application documents: (a) the internal organizational context, (b) the external organizational context, (c) the strategic planning process, (d) strategy considerations, (e) action plan development and deployment, (f) results, and (g) performance measurement.

The organizational context was the starting point of the investigation. The application documents describe the organization's internal and external contexts, including key characteristics and relationships as well as influences and challenges.

More importantly, the information in the applications portrays the strategic context of the organization and the strategic direction it wishes to take (NIST, 2011). The context helps to identify what is relevant for each case.

The strategic planning process and the interrelated consideration of strategic factors determine the organization's strategic objectives. The application documents depict the creation of strategies and present the applied systems and methods for achieving performance excellence, stimulating innovation, building knowledge and capabilities, and creating sustainability (Latham & Vinyard, 2008). The CPEF guides the presentation of the applied strategic processes and offers insights into the formulation of the strategic objectives process (NIST, 2011). The strategic objectives interconnect the strategic process with the action development and deployment process.

The action development and deployment processes investigate the operational effort to translate strategic objectives into concrete action. The development and deployment of action plans is a reiterative exercise employing feedback loops to continually revise the strategic process, the strategic objectives, and the action plan development and deployment (NIST, 2011). The cycle concludes in performance projections, which set standards and objectives for the desired outcomes of the operational conduct.

The results consider the organization's performance and improvements in all key areas, including customer-focused outcomes, workforce-focused outcomes, leadership and governance outcomes, and financial or market driven results (Calhoun, 2002). The results also compare achieved performance levels to those of competitors and other organizations with comparable product offerings (NIST, 2011). This requires that actual results be measured as a precondition for establishing cross-comparisons.

The measurement concept is an integral tool of performance strategies. In the Baldrige model, performance measurement is examined in terms of how organizations choose, collect, analyze, and manage data to improve their performance (NIST, 2011). Performance excellence strategies must contain key information about effectively measuring and analyzing performance to drive improvement and organizational competitiveness (Calhoun, 2002). The measurement function is the central tool used to align the organization's operations with its strategic objectives. It combines information about effectively measuring, analyzing, and improving performance and managing organizational knowledge to fuel improvement and organizational competitiveness (NIST, 2011). This "brain activity" guides the organization's process management, helping it to achieve key organizational results and strategic objectives and also anticipate and respond to changes (Calhoun, 2002).

These seven factors are integrated in the CPEF, building a foundation for evaluation and feedback and providing a framework for diagnosing the organization's overall performance management system. The CPEF itself is designed in a way that is specific in describing the integral aspects of organizational excellence, but flexible enough to leave room for interpretation. In other words, the CPEF does not specify how organizational excellence should be attained; rather, it serves as the basis for evaluating and giving feedback and provides a framework for diagnosing any organization's overall perform-ance management system (Calhoun, 2002). This framework introduces a con-ceptual commonality among the areas addressed in the applications and ensures a high standard in the documentation.

The program's standards are met through a stringent application review performed by the Board of Examiners, which consists of an independent re-view by members and a team review led by a senior or alumni examiner (Cal-houn, 2002). High scoring organizations also receive site visits. The final review and recommendation of awards is the responsibility of the Panel of Judges (NIST, 2011).

The review process ensures the convergence of results and enhances con-fidence in the findings (Eisenhardt, 1989; Eisenhardt & Graebner, 2007). Con-sequently, the application documents offer rich qualitative data on the real world application of the strategic management process in the business context. However, working with the application documents requires a researcher to in-terpret the implications of the data. The degree to which the study provides meaning by noting patterns or inconsistencies in the evidence relies on the quality of the data analysis within the limitations of the conceptual framework and the research questions (Hodder, 1994).

Sources of Data

This study uses only publicly available secondary data for the analysis. Consequently, there are no issues of informed consent of the participants. The financial data came from the EDGAR database via the U.S. Securities and Ex-change Commission and from the Fundamentals Quarterly file on the COM-PUSTAT North American database, which is available through the Wharton Research Data Services (WRDS) website. Then, individual queries were con-structed based on the four digit SIC code for the selected NQA winning firms. The time period selected was for a total of five years of quarterly data. This includes five full years of performance data before the award year, five full years after their award, and the year of the award itself. The queries were constructed selecting for the following data elements in the Fundamentals Quarterly data file (see Table

Table 5

Elements of Data Queries in COMPUSTAT

Company Performance Data Element	COMPUSTAT Code
Current assets	ACTQ
Total assets	ATQ
Earnings per share, diluted, including extraordinary items EPSFIQ	
Current liabilities	LCTQ
Total liabilities	LTQ
Net income	NIQ
Net Sales	SALEQ

Data Analysis

Statistical Approach

Both before and after the award of an NQA in order to answer the first research question. In order to answer the research question, r-tests were used to compare the performance of NQA winning firms against their key competitors. The rationale for using I-test is that the sample size is less than 30 and the i-test compares population means, which, in turn, answers the research questions (Doane & Seward, 2007).

The shape and symmetry of the data was examined using the skewness and kurtosis measures. The skewness is a measure of the symmetry of the data and data with normal symmetry should approximate zero. A skewness factor of greater than zero indicates a positive skew with more data points above the median. A skewness of less than zero indicates a negative skew with more data points below the median. Similarly, the kurtosis is a measure of the peak of the data, and for normal data, it should approximate zero. A positive kurtosis measure indicates a data set that has a relatively high peak in the middle, whereas a kurtosis below zero indicates a relatively flat data set ("NIST/SEMATECH e-Handbook of Statistical Methods," 2006).

To confirm the observation made through probability plot, a statistical test procedure is used to test the normality of the data and the p-value, indicating whether the null hypothesis is rejected or not. The null hypothesis for this is H0: The data follows normal distribution the alternate hypothesis is H1: The data do not follow normal distribution. This test is used because, "the probability plot has the attraction of revealing discrepancies between the sample and the hypothesized distribution, and it is usually easy to spot outliers" (Doane & Seward, 2007, p. 685). The test procedure is known as the Anderson-Darling test and is a popular test procedure for testing the normality of the data. This test procedure gives a graphical presentation along with the test statistic value and the p-value. This p-value indicates whether the null hypothesis is rejected or not.

Since a 5% level of significance is being used, if this p-value is less than 0.05, the null hypothesis is rejected; otherwise, it is not rejected. In other words, if the p-value of the test is less than 0.05, it means that the data do not follow normal distribution, and if it is more than 0.05, then it can be concluded that the data follow normal distribution patterns at 5% level of significance.

Validity and Reliability

Sharpe and Koperwas (2003) identified two dimensions of validity: internal and external. Internal validity is the assurance that alternative explanations may be ruled out, and that the proposed explanation is indeed, valid. External validity, on the other hand, is the ability to generalize the explanation to applications outside of the immediate use.

That is, the ability of a practitioner to apply the concept outside the field of the original testing, for instance, into a real world setting.

Internal validity was assured in this study by using the most direct metric available to measure firm performance (Sharpe & Koperwas, 2003). Hypothesis addressed this perspective. The actual financial performance results that were auditable were reported to the U.S. Securities and Exchange Commission. Short of intentional fraud in the reporting of these measures, these are the most direct and reliable measures of firm performance available

To assure a higher degree of external validity, hypothesis compared performance between the NQA-winning firms and their key competitors. This serves to provide an outside application of the results into the context of the applicable market segment to ensure the generalizability of the construct. The second set of hypotheses is concerned with the interaction of the experimental treatment with other factors and the "ability to generalize to (and across) times, settings, or persons" (Cooper & Schindler, 2003, p.434). This would address questions that shareholders of firms that have not initiated Baldrige management practices may have regarding the value of those initiatives.

In addition to the proactive approach to validity described previously, caution was used regarding the threats to validity outlined by Creswell (2003). Internal threats are associated with "procedures, treatments, or experiences of the participants" (p. 171) that threatens the conclusions drawn by the researcher. In the secondary data, the latter two threats are not germane. However, the first internal threat, that of a procedural threat, is possible. To mitigate this threat, the statistical techniques used are all fundamental, sound, and well established statistical techniques, widely used and described. This threat is possible, but any comparisons between companies are being made within the confines of the market segment as defined by the applicable SIC code and within the same time period of study.

One final consideration on the issue of validity is construct validity as described by Katzer, Cook, and Crouch (1998), "that the concept (under study) is being measured and not something else" (p. 102). As stated previously, since the metrics are the foundational financial and operating performance measures of a business, there is no more direct measure than the ones being used. As stated earlier in this study, these are the central measure of efficiency of how the firm used its assets (resources) to generate net income and, consequently, profit.

The reliability of a study can be affected by noise, or random error, in measurement, "it is also repeatable and stable" (Katzer et al., 1998, p. 98). Reliability also refers to the trustworthiness and dependability of the data. Cooper and Schindler (2003) stated that reliability is "the degree to which a measurement is free of random or unstable error" (p. 236), noting that it has three components: stability, equivalence, and internal consistency. Stability is the ability to obtain consistent results from measurement. Equivalence is concerned with "variation at one point in time among observers and samples of items" (p. 238).

The credibility of the research centers on the trustworthiness of the study (Morrow, 2005). This study made use of MBNQA application documents. The MBNQA promotes organizational excellence by sharing information on the successful application of the CPEF in award winning organizations. Independent, trained, and qualified expert groups review the published application documents objectively. The layered review process not only ensures the reliability of the data, but also establishes a high level of rigor throughout the data collection and presentation process (Gasson, 2004). The application documents provide a comprehensive representation of the fact-based strategic management process in leading edge organizations.

During the data analysis process, the researcher transcribed the observed findings into meta-matrices. This process seeks to maintain the trustworthiness of the data while providing further insight into the prevailing configurations and temporal arrangements of factors and relevant elements in the metrics-based strategic management process (Campbell & Shiller, 1986). Thus, when combined, the application documents and the transcribed information created an internally coherent research ground, building a systematic, context-rich, and meaningful framework for the study's emerging concepts and theories (Denzin, 1989).

The study needs to allow for transferability as well. To this end, the researcher took a multi-case research approach, employing a sample of MBNQA recipients in the sectors of manufacturing, small business, and service. Multi-case research approaches lead to the recognition of patterns of relationships among constructs within and across cases and their underlying logical arguments. Transferability requires a theoretical validity that can be applied or transferred to alternative settings (Becker, 1990; Bogdan & Biklen, 1992). The cross-case study approach allowed for the replication, contrasting, and extending of the findings across cases. It uses case data, emerging theory, and existing literature. The resulting interrelation of qualitative evidence and deductive research in a theory building multiple-case study research design was used to produce rich and meaningful concepts and established the basis for transferability.

Transferability also relates to generalizability. Generalizability assesses concepts in terms of their applicability to other theory networks beyond the immediate scope of a particular study (Kennedy, 1988; Maxwell, 1992). This research employed multiple case studies to create empirical descriptions of data-driven decision-making in high performing organizations. The case-specific findings replicated, contrasted, and extended across cases. Recognizing patterns or relationships among aspects within and across cases and their underlying arguments allowed the emerging theory to be applied to other theory networks.

In sum, the determination and composition of the sample, the setting, and the study design enhanced the transferability and the generalizability of the study results (LeCompte & Preissle, 1993; Lincoln & Guba, 1985). Criteria dependability and confirmability require consistency throughout the study (Miles & Huberman, 1994). The multi-case study design enhances this by making assumptions and conclusions in the context of the primary data (Goetz & LeCompte, 1984). The structured review process for the application documents ensures quality data with a high degree of stability over time and across documents (Eisenhardt & Graebner, 2007). In addition, all data was transcribed into a meta-matrix analysis sheet. Arguably, this procedural stability enhances the dependability and conformability of the data across cases.

Notwithstanding the strength of the data, research was ineffectual unless the data analysis was closely monitored. It is therefore necessary to critically assess the potential for bias. Biases may affect the research; they may surface in the form of the researcher's unawareness of his/her bias or unacknowledged lack of neutrality (Miles & Huberman, 1994). To control for researcher bias and lack of neutrality, the study describes explicitly and in detail the general methods and procedures used. To limit the exposure to researcher bias, independent expert knowledge was obtained (Guba & Lincoln, 1989; Mertens, 2010). In short, this study meets the core requirements of qualitative research.

Ethical Considerationsl

This research investigated the strategic process of MBNQA organizations by examining publicly available secondary data. It does not require the direct involvement of participants. As a result, there is no immediate risk of exposure to any study subjects. Nevertheless, the rightness or wrongness of research extends beyond sampling; research ethics are crucial in every aspect of an investigation (Clegg & Slife, 2009). Therefore, this research adhered strictly to the Institutional Review Board (IRB) process and the policies and procedures of Argosy University. These policies and procedures emphasize the need for justice and respect as guiding principles of scientific research. To ensure adherence to the principles of ethical research, this study ensured privacy, confidentiality, and anonymity for the study objects. For this purpose, the application documents and the associated data from the cases was coded to prevent disclosing the names of the participating organizations. As a result, the study did not reveal identifying information associated with the findings, nor the findings identify any of the studied subjects.

Summary

This chapter outlined the methodological and statistical analysis approach to be used for this study. It specified the types of statistical tests to be used and gave a justification for their implementation. The method of population selection and the sources of the data were identified. It was also noted that because of a small size of the population, statistical sampling techniques were not used for the analyses procedures. All the NQA-winning firms were studied and then their performance was compared to a portfolio of their key competitors. The source of these data was the firm's 10-K/10-Q financial reports located in the U.S. Securities and Exchange Commission's EDGAR database.

Chapter Four uses the statistical techniques illustrated in this chapter to gather and analyze subjects' performance data in a two-step approach. First, the data was examined to determine if it displays normal distribution. If it does, then the parametric techniques described previously was used. If it appears to display non-normal distribution, then the previously mentioned nonparametric techniques was used.

CHAPTER FOUR: RESULTS

Restatement of the Purpose

The purpose of this research was to examine if winning the MBQNA has a significant effect on firm performance, as measured by ROA. Measures of financial performance for a sample of MBNQA winners from 2004-2015 were analyzed to answer the research question and test the study hypotheses.

In this chapter, the results of the statistical analysis are presented. First, a description of the firms in the sample is presented, followed by a statistical description of the performance measures for the firms in the sample, which included ROA, ROE, EVA, and MVA. Next, the results of the assessment of the assumptions of linear regression and dependent samples I test are presented. Following the results of the assumption testing, the results of the hypothesis testing are presented. Finally, the results of the auxiliary analysis conducted to further examine the relationships between winning the MBNQA and firm performance are presented.

Description of the Sample

The sample was composed of firms that had won and not won the MBNQA during the period 2004-2015. Among the firms in the sample, those that did not win the MBNQA {M— 131,699.00, SD — 112,628.42) tended to have fewer employees than those who did win the MBNQA {M— 1,572,645.94, SD — 6,023,931.89). Firms that had not won the MBNQA also differed from firms that had won the MBNQA in price/sales and competitor price/sales. Among firms that had not won the MBNQA, both firms in the dataset and their competitors, price/sales {M — .02, SD — .01) was lower than for firms that had won the MBNQA in the dataset (M— .11, SD — .40) and their competitors {M—.02, SD — .01). The central tendency of the characteristics of the firms in the dataset and their competitors by whether the firm won the MBNQA is presented in Table 6.

	Employees, Price/Sales, and Competitor Price/Sales					
	No Win		Won		Total	
Variable	M	SD	M	SD	M	SD
Employees	131,699.00	112,628.42	1,572,645.94	6,023,931.89	1,092,330.29	4,914,392.69
Price/Sales	.02	.01	.11	.40	.09	.33
Competitor Price/Sales		.01	.02	.01 .02	.02	.01

Table 6. Central Tendency of Number of Employees, Price/Sales, and Competitor Price Sales

The central tendency of ROA during the period 2004-2015 for the firms in the dataset appeared to vary with whether the firm won the MBNQA. However, the results of the hypothesis testing indicated that this effect was not statistically significant.

Overall, average ROA during the period 2004-2015 was larger for firms that did not win the MBNQA {M — .25, SD — .30) than it was for firms that

	Returns on Assets 2004-2015					
	No Win		WON		Total	
Variable	M	SD	M	SD	M	SD
ROA2015	.09	.05	.09	.03	.09	.04
ROA2014	.09	.05	.17	.22	.15	.18
ROA2013	.17	.17	.25	.57	.23	.48
ROA2012	.17	.16	.17	.59	.17	.49
ROA2011	.26	.32	.08	.35	.13	.34
ROA2010	.36	.52	.07	.33	.15	.40
ROA2009	.35	.56	.04	.41	.13	.46
ROA2008	.77	1.34	.07	.16	.28	.76
ROA2007	.26	.26	.13	il	.17	.17
ROA2006	.24	.22	.12	.09	.16	.14
ROA2005	.14	.09	.11	.07	.12	.07
ROA2004	.11	.09	.09	.06	.09	.07
Total Avg. ROA	.25	.30	.11	.26	.15	.27

Table 7. Central Tendency of Returns on Assets by MBNQA Winner During 2004-2015

did win the MBNQA {M —.11, SD — .26). The central tendency of ROA during the period 2004-2015 is presented in Table 7.

The central tendency of ROE during the period 2004-2015 for the firms in the dataset appeared to vary with whether the firm won the MBNQA. However, unlike the findings for ROA, average ROE was larger for firms that won the MBNQA {M——.34, SD = .23) than it was for firms that did not win the MBNQA {M—.18, SD — .08). Based on the findings of the linear regression on ROE presented in the Auxiliary Analysis section, this difference was also not statistically significant. The central tendency of ROE during the period 2004-2015 is presented in Table 8.

	Returns on Earnings 2004-2015					
	NoWin		Won		Total	
Variable	M	SD	M	SD	M	SD
ROE2015	.32	.22	.47	.54	.41	.42
ROE2014	.19	.12	.28	.34	.25	.29
ROE2013	.18	.12	.50	.90	.41	.76
ROE2012	.15	.08	.46	.51	.37	.45
ROE2011	.16	.06	.35	.24	.29	.22
ROE2010	.17	.10	.31	.21	.27	.19
ROE2009	.03	.24	.31	.27	.23	.29
ROE2008	.15	.31	.28	.12	.24	.19
ROE2007	.23	.11	.31	.12	.28	.12
ROE2006	.24	.11	.26	.11	.25	.11
ROE2005	.21	.09	.23	.09	.22	.09
ROE2004	.16	.13	.21	.09	.20	.11
Total Avg.ROE	.18	.08	.34	.23	.29	.20

Table 8. Central Tendency of Return on Earnings by MBNQA Winner During 2004-2015

As was the case in the central tendency of total average ROA for the firms in the dataset, average EVA tended to vary with whether the firm won the MBNQA. Average EVA was larger for firms that did not win the MBNQA [M — .37, SD — .49) than it was for firms that did win the MBNQA {M— .15, SD — .08). Although average EVA was more than twice as large for the firms that did not win the MBNQA, the effect of winning the MBNQA on EVA was tested and found to not be statistically significant, indicating that the difference in EVA is not statistically significant. The central tendency of EVA during the period 2004-2015 is presented in Table 9.Similar to the central tendency of ROA and EVA for the firms in the dataset, average MVA tended to vary with

| | Economic Value Added 2004-2015 | | | | | |
| | No Win | | Won | | Total | |
Variable	M	SD	M	SD	M	SD
EVA2015	.14	.05	.13	.03	.13	.03
EVA2014	.21	.10	.15	.10	.17	.10
EVA2013	2.81	5.92	.15	.06	.93	3.21
EVA2012	.13	.08	.15	.10	.14	.09
EVA2011	.16	.15	.16	.07	.16	.09
EVA2010	.22	.22	.16	.08	.18	.13
EVA2009	.14	.19	.16	.09	.15	.12
EVA2008	.11	.15	.15	.08	.14	.10
EVA2007	.12	.07	.17	.09	.15	.08
EVA2006	.14	.06	.17	.09	.16	.08
EVA2005	.12	.05	.14	.09	.14	.08
EVA2004	.09	.08	.16	.10	.14	.10
Total Avg. EVA	.37	.49	.15	.08	.21	.27

Table 9. Central Tendency of Economic Value Added by MBNQA Winner During 2004-2015

whether the firm won the MBNQA. Average MVA was also larger for firms that did not win the MBNQA {M — .22, SD — .30) than it was for firms that did not the MBNQA {M— .10, SD — .08). Like the measures of central tendency for EVA, the measures of central tendency for MVA were more than twice as large for the firms that did not win the MBNQA. This relationship was also tested and found to not be statistically significant, indicating that the difference in MVA among firms that won the MBNQA and did not win the MBNQA was not statistically significant. The central tendency of MVA during the period 2004-2015 is presented in Table 10.

| Variable | Market Value Added 2004-2015 | | | | | |
| | No Win | | Won | | Total | |
	M	SD	M	SD	M	SD
MVA2015	.07	.05	.10	.03	.09	.04
MVA2014	.38	.66	.08	.06	.17	.36
MVA2013	.40	.66	.07	.05	.17	.37
MVA2012	.46	.87	.07	.06	.19	.47
MVA2011	.07	.03	.07	.05	.07	.04
MVA2010	.003	.19	.07	.05	.05	.1i
MVA2009	-.01	.14	.09	.53	.06	.45
MVA2008	.14	.23	.05	.04	.08	.13
MVA2007	.49	.82	.06	.04	.18	.46
MVA2006	.15	.08	.17	.39	.16	.33
MVA2005	.17	.13	.16	.40	.17	.34
MVA2004	.28	.44	.20	.37	.22	.38
Total Avg. MVA	.22	.30	.10	.08	.13	.17

Table 10. Central Tendency of MVA by MBNQA Winner During 2004-2015

Assumption Testing

Two statistical tests were utilized for this study: the linear regression and the dependent samples r test. The assumptions of these tests were assessed to gauge the generalizability of the findings. For the linear regressions, three assumptions are typically assessed: normality, linearity, and homoscedasticity. However, since the only independent variable in four of the linear regression was dichotomous, the assumptions of linearity and homoscedasticity were not assessed for those four linear regressions. For the dependent samples it I test, the assumption of normality was assessed for each of the four measures of firm performance (ROA, ROE, EVA, and MVA) both pre-MBNQA and post-MBNQA. To assess the normality of the variables used in the analysis, histograms of the frequency distribution of the variables were examined for a bell-shaped curve. To assess the assumptions of linearity and homoscedasticity, a scatterplot of the standardized residuals against the standardized predicted

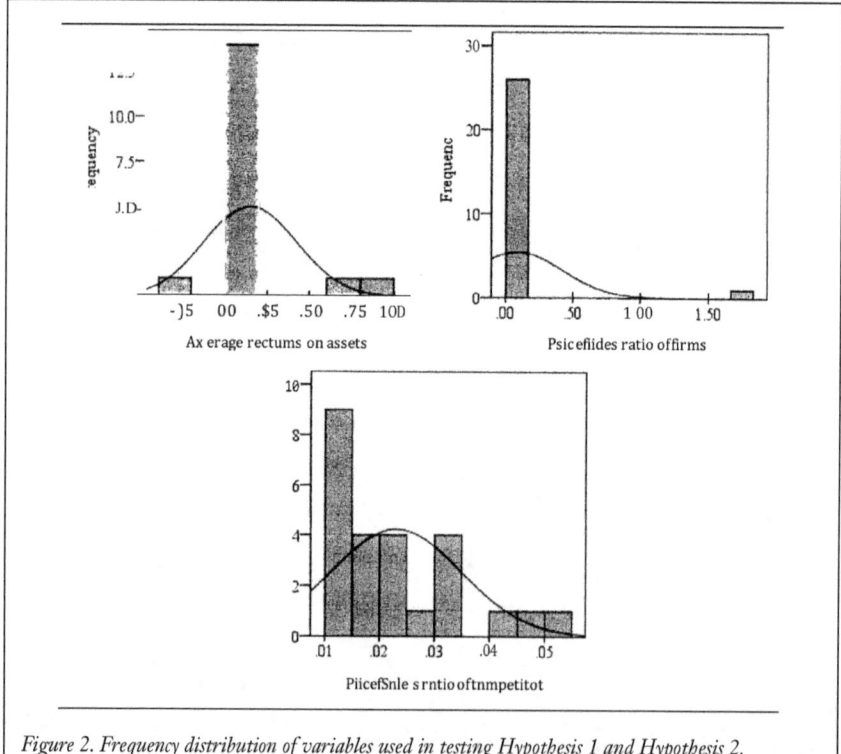

Figure 2. Frequency distribution of variables used in testing Hypothesis 1 and Hypothesis 2.

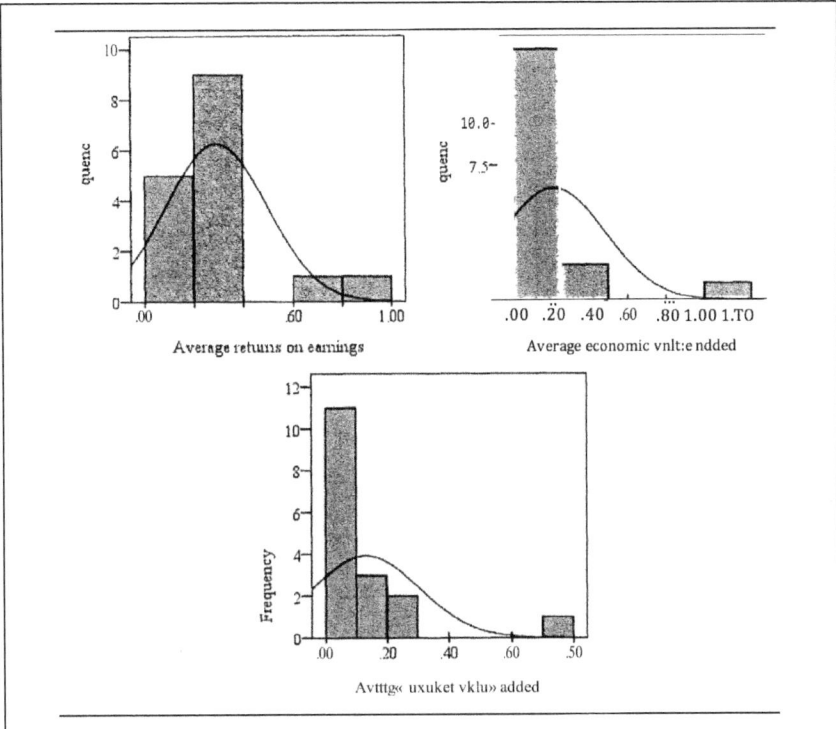

Figure 3. Frequency distribution of variables used in testing returns on earnings, economic value added, and market value added.

values found in the output for each of the linear regressions.

After examining histograms of the frequency distribution of the study variables, the distributions were found to deviate from a bell-shaped curve and were not normally distributed. Square root, natural logarithm, and common logarithm data transformations were attempted to aid in meeting the assumption of normality. However, the transformations did not improve the distributions enough to warrant the use of the transformed variables in the analyses. Therefore, the original distributions were used in the analyses. The histograms of the frequency distributions of the variables used in the hypothesis testing are presented in Figure 2. The histograms of the variables used in the auxiliary statistical analysis are presented in Figures 3-5.

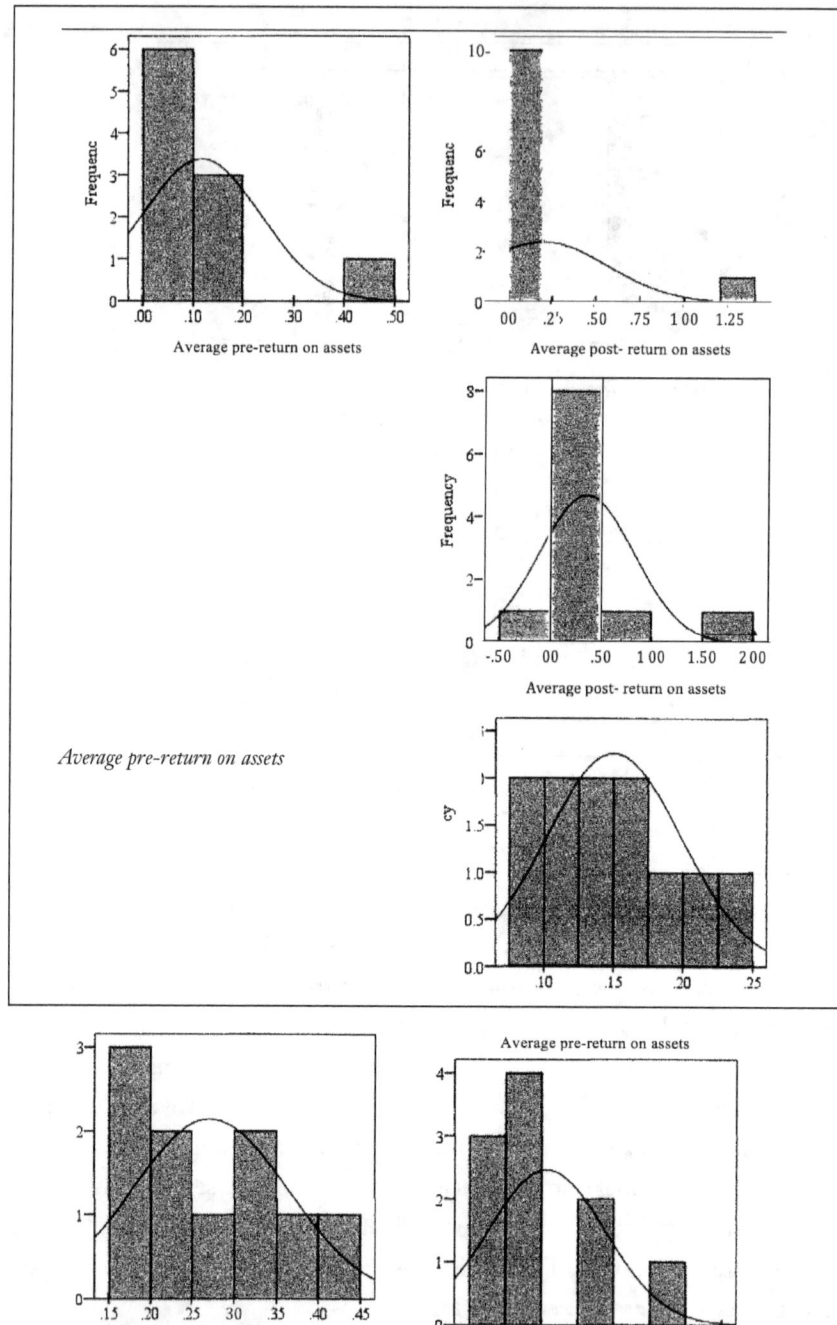

Figure 4. Frequency distribution of variables used in I tests on returns on assets, returns on earnings, and economic value added.

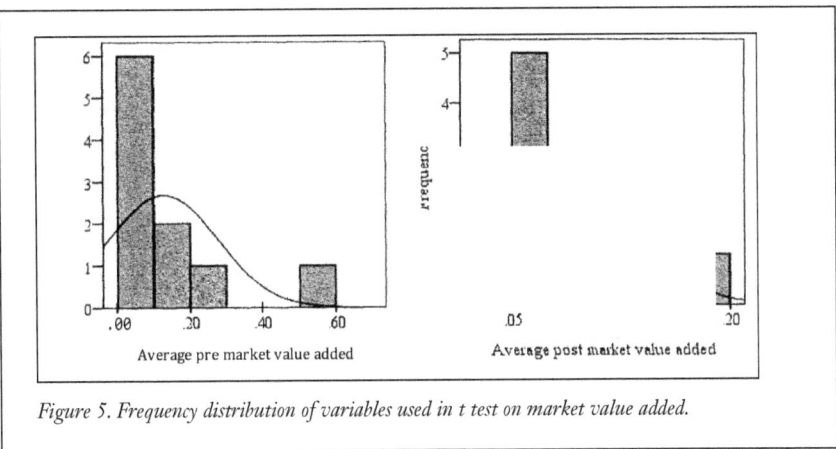

Figure 5. Frequency distribution of variables used in t test on market value added.

The assumptions of linearity and homoscedasticity were assessed for the multiple regression conducted to test Hypothesis 2. If the distribution of points in the scatterplot had formed a curve, the assumption of linearity would have been violated, and if the distribution of points in the scatterplot had formed a cone or a funnel at either end of the distribution, the assumption of homoscedasticity would have been violated. This was not the case, and the assumptions of linearity and homoscedasticity were considered met for the multiple regression conducted to test Hypothesis 2. The scatterplot of the standardized residuals against the standardized predicted values is presented in Figure 6.

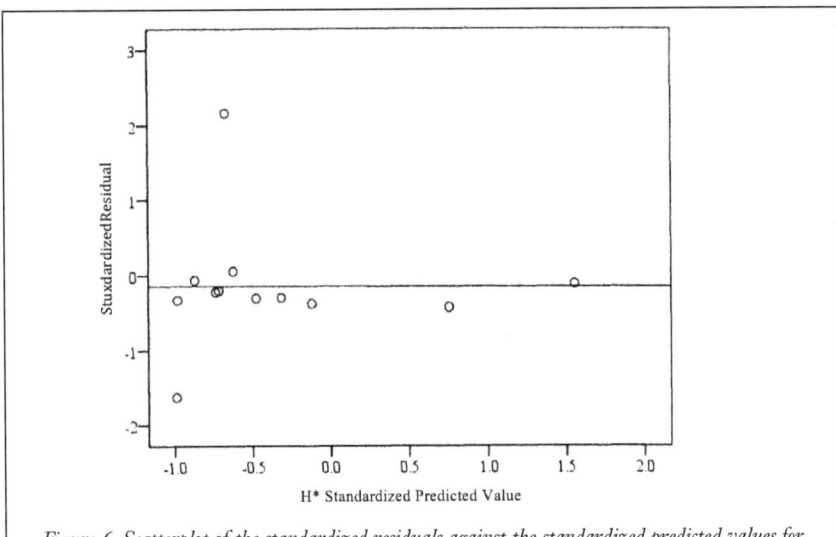

Figure 6. Scatterplot of the standardized residuals against the standardized predicted values for the multiple linear regression conducted to test Hypothesis 2.

69

Hypothesis Testing

Hypothesis 1

HU. BROA/ 0 where BRoA is the slope of the linear line representing the relationship between winning the MBNQA and firm performance.

To test Hypothesis 1 that there is not a relationship between winning the MBNQA and firm performance, a linear regression was conducted. The independent variable in the linear regression was the dichotomous variable representing whether the firm in the dataset won the MBNQA (0 — the firm did not win the MBNQA during the period 2004- 2015 and 1 = the firm did win the MBNQA during the period 2004-2015). The dependent variable in the linear regression was the interval level variable representing average ROA during the period 2004-2015 for each of the firms in the dataset. The results of the linear regression were not statistically significant,(1, 15) = .96, p — .34, and indicated that winning the MBNQA accounted for 6% r squared of the variability in ROA during the period 2004-2015. These findings indicated that winning the MBNQA did not have a statistically significant effect on the performance of the firms in the dataset as measured by ROA. In Table 11, the results from the linear regression to test Hypothesis 1 are presented.

Linear Regression Analysis Using MBNQA Outcome to Predict ROA

	Predicting Returns on Assets		
Variable	B	SE	95% CI
Constant	.25	.12	(-.005, .50)
Dichotomized MBNQA	-.13	.14	(-.42, .16)
e'	.06		
F	.96		

Note. n — 17. CI = confidence interval.

Table 11. Linear Regression Analysis Using MBNQA Outcome to Predict ROA.

Hypothesis 2

To test Hypothesis 2 that there is not a relationship between winning the indicators of number of employees, the price to sales ratio of the firm, and the price to sales ratio of the competing firm, a regression was conducted. The independent variables in the linear regression were the interval level variables representing the number of employees in the firm, the price to sales ratio of the firm, and the price to sales ratio of the competing firm. The dependent variable in the regression was the interval level variable representing average ROA during the period 2004-2015 for each of the firms in the dataset. The results of the regression were not statistically significant, $(3, 8) = .18$, $p - .91$, and indicated that the combination of the variables representing the number of employees in the firm, the price to sales ratio of the firm, and the price to sales ratio of the competing firm accounted for 6.3% of the variability in ROA during the period 2004- 2015. These findings indicated that the combination of the variables representing the number of employees in the firm, the price to sales ratio of the firm, and the price to sales ratio did not have a statistically significant effect on the performance of the firms in the dataset as measured by ROA. The results from the linear regression analysis for Hypothesis 2 are presented in Table 12.

	Employees and Price/Sales Predicting Returns on Assets		
Variable	B	SE	95% CI
Constant	.11	.20	(-.34, .56)
Price/Sales Ratio	-.01	.27	(-.62, .61)
Price/Sales Ratio Competitor	1.77	7.68	(-15.61, 19.15)
R^2		.006	
X		.03	

Note. $n - 12$. CI = confidence interval.

Table 12.Linear Regression Analysis Using the Number of Employees, Price/Sales Ratio, and Price/Sales Ratio of Competing Firm to Predict ROA

Auxiliary Analysis

Although the results of the hypothesis testing was not statistically significant, additional statistical analysis was conducted to further examine the relationship between winning the MBNQA and firm performance. In addition to ROA, three other measures of firm performance were analyzed: ROE, EVA, and MVA. The relationship between these measures of firm performance and winning the MBNQA were analyzed by conducting three linear regressions. Following these three linear regressions, differences in the four measures of firm performance after winning the MBNQA were examined by conducting four dependent samples r tests.

Regression Using Returns on Earnings

To examine the relationship between winning the MBNQA and firm performance as measured by ROE, a linear regression was conducted. The independent variable in the linear regression was the dichotomous variable representing whether the firm in the dataset won the MBNQA (0 — the firm did not win the MBNQA during the period 2004- 2015 and 1 = the firm did win the MBNQA during the period 2004-2015). The dependent variable in the linear regression was the interval level variable representing average ROE during the period 2004-2015 for each of the firms in the dataset. The results of the linear regression were not statistically significant,(1, 14) = 2.28, p — .15, and indicated that winning the MBNQA accounted for 14% of the variability in ROE during the period 2004-2015. These findings indicated that winning the MBNQA did not have a statistically significant effect on the performance of the firms in the dataset as measured by ROE. These results were similar to those for the regression conducted on ROA. However, winning the MBNQA had a greater effect on ROE than ROA and accounted for more than twice the variability in ROE. In Table 13, the results from the regression on ROE are presented.

	Predicting Returns on Earnings		
Variable	B	SE	95% CI
Constant	.18	.09	(-.004, .37)
Dichotomized MBNQA	.15	.10	(-.06, .37)
R^2		.14	
F		2.28	

Note. n — 16. CI = confidence interval.

Table 13. Linear Regression Analysis Using MBNQA Outcome to Predict ROE

Regression Using Economic Value Added

To examine the relationship between winning the MBNQA and firm performance as measured by EVA, a linear regression was estimated. The independent variable in the linear regression was the dichotomous variable representing whether the firm in the dataset won the MBNQA (0 = the firm did not win the MBNQA during the period 2004- 2015 and 1 = the firm did win the MBNQA during the period 2004-2015). The dependent variable in the linear regression was the interval level variable representing average EVA during the period 2004-2015 for each of the firms in the dataset. The results of the linear regression were not statistically significant,(1, 15) — 2.49, p — .14, and indicated that winning the MBNQA accounted for 14.2% of the variability in EVA during the period 2004-2015. These findings indicated that winning the MBNQA did not have a statistically significant effect on the performance of the firms in the dataset as measured by EVA. These results were similar to those for the regression conducted on ROE. However, as was the case in the regression on ROE, winning the MBNQA had a greater effect on EVA than on both ROA and ROE. The results from the linear regression on EVA are presented in Table 14.

	Predicting Economic Value Added		
Variable	B	SE	95% CI
Constant	.36	.11	(.12, .60)
Dichotomized MBNQA	-.21	.13	(-.48, .07)
2		.142	
F		2.49	

Note. n — 17. CI = confidence interval.

Table 14. Linear Regression Analysis Using MBNQA Outcome to Predict Economic Value Added

Regression Using Market Value Addeds

To examine the relationship between winning the MBNQA and firm performance as measured by MVA, a linear regression was conducted. The independent variable in the linear regression was the dichotomous variable representing whether the firm in the dataset won the MBNQA (0 = the firm did not win the MBNQA during the period 2004- 2015 and 1 - the firm did win the MBNQA during the period 2004-2015). The dependent variable in the linear regression was the interval level variable representing average MVA during the period 2004-2015 for each of the firms in the dataset. The results of the linear regression were not statistically significant,(1, 15) = 1.73, p — .21, and indicated that winning the MBNQA accounted for 10.3% of the variability in MVA during the period 2004-2015. These findings indicated that winning the MBNQA did not have a statistically significant effect on the performance of the firms in the dataset as measured by MVA. These results were similar to those for the regressions conducted on ROA, ROE, and EVA. However, as was the case in the regression on ROE, winning the MBNQA had a greater effect on MVA than on ROA but not as large as the effect on ROE and EVA. The results of the linear regression on MVA are presented in Table 15.

	Predicting Market Value Added		
Variable	B	SE	95% CI
Constant	.21	.07	(.06, .37)
Dichotomized MBNQA	-.11	.08	(-.29, .07)
R^2		.142	
F		2.49	

Note. n — 17. CI = confidence interval.

Table 15. Linear Regression Analysis Using MBNQA Outcome to Predict Market Value Added

Dependent Samples t Tests on the Four Measures of Firm Performance

To examine whether the performance of the firms in the dataset was improved after winning the MBNQA, four dependent samples t tests were conducted on each of the four measures of firm performance: ROA, ROE, EVA, and MVA. To create the variables that were used in the analyses, ROA, ROE, EVA, and MVA scores were averaged for the period before winning the MBNQA and for the period after winning the MBNQA.

1. The results of the first dependent samples r test on ROA was not statistically significant, r (9) = -1.06, p — .32, indicating that there was not a statistically significant difference between ROA before winning the MBNQA {M —— .12, SD —.12) and ROA after winning the MBNQA {M— .21, SD — .38).

2. The results of the second dependent samples t test on ROE was not statistically significant, i (9) = -.78, p — .46, indicating that there was not a statistically significant difference between ROE before winning the MBNQA {M —— .27, SD —.09) and ROE after winning the MBNQA {M — .38, SD — .49).

3. The results of the third dependent samples t test on EVA was not statistically significant, i (9) — .46, p — .66, indicating that there was not a statistically significant difference between EVA before winning the MBNQA {M —— .16, SD —.08) and EVA after winning the MBNQA {M— .15, SD — .05).

4. The results of the fourth dependent samples I test on MVA was not statistically significant, r (9) — .71, p — .50, indicating that there was not
a statistically significant difference between MVA before winning the
MBNQA {M— .13, SD —.15) and MVA after winning the MBNQA
{M— .09, SD — .05). The results of the four dependent samples r tests
are presented in Table 16.

	PreMBNQA		PostMBNQA				95% CI	
Variable	*M*	*SD*	*M*	*SD*	I (9)	*p*	*LL*	*UL*
ROA	.12	.12	.21	.38	-1.06	.32	-.30	.11
ROE	.27	.09	.38	.49	-.78	.46	-.41	.20
EVA	.16	.08	.15	.05	.46	.66	-.03	.05
MVA	.13	.15	.09	.05	.71	.50	-.08	.15

Note. n — 10. CI — confidence interval.

Table 16. Linear Regression Analysis Using MBNQA Outcome to Predict Economic Value Added

Summary

In this chapter, the results of the statistical analysis were presented. The
results indicated that although firms that had not won the MBNQA during
the period of 2004- 2015 outperformed other firms in ROA, EVA, and MVA
during the same period, winning the MBNQA did not significantly affect
ROA, ROE, EVA, or MVA. Furthermore, there was not a statistically significant difference in ROA, ROE, EVA, or MVA prior to winning the MBNQA
and after winning the MBNQA. This indicated that although average ROA,
ROE, EVA, and MVA varied by whether the firm had won the MBNQA, either
the sample size or the difference were not large enough for the variations to
be statistically significant. In Chapter Five, the findings and their implications
on the pursuit of the MBNQA by firm leaders will be discussed, conclusions
will be drawn from the findings, and recommendations will be made for future
research based on the findings from this study.

CHAPTER FIVE: SUMMARY, FINDINGS, CONCLUSIONS, AND RECOMMENDATION

Summary

Many organizations believe in authenticity and value of national quality awards (NQAs), such as the Malcolm Baldrige National Quality Award (Cazzell & Ulmer, 2009; Hladchencko, 2015). Organizations assume the bestowing of such an award has a powerful effect on financial returns and earnings, leading organizations to spend a great deal of time and money toward the accomplishment of the award's receipt. In spite of this, the amount of time and money spent on working toward the obtainment of an award are never a true picture of the performance of the organization (Gorelick, 2004; Forma, 2012; Jacob, Madu, & Tang, 2004). Studies have been conducted to determine whether the winning of such an award adds value to firms and to the investors in the firm (Jacob, Madu, & Tang, 2012).

The purpose of this study was to demonstrate the importance of understanding, in detail, the link between the performances of the business and the quality improvement initiatives that are set forth by NQAs. Elements of quality taken into account include levels of customer satisfaction, quality metrics, defect rates, cycle times, and allowing for a greater understanding of the role that quality has in increased competitive advantage.

In turn, the bestowing of a NQA like the MBNQA occurs (Kotler, 2000, 2012; Chong & Rundus, 2004; Griffith et al., 2012). The MBNQA is an award of particularly high prestige, created by President Ronald Regan in 1987 (MBNQA, n.d.). The MBNQA looks at the total quality management of the organization, requiring the organization to continually improve its performance, which in turn, allows the organization to increase its overall competitiveness.

There has been increased concern that the winning of a MBNQA does not serve as a measure of a firm's performance, and the performance of the firm is not improved by the receipt of the award, rather the striving for the award serves as the means of increasing the firm's overall performance, acting as an antecedent to winning the MBNQA. In other words, there is no clear indication or convincing evidence that winning the award results in higher performance by the organization (Van der Laan et al., 2009; Sabella et al., 2014).

The study attempted to determine whether winning the MBNQA improves firm performance or whether firm performance is an antecedent to winning the MBNQA. In order to accomplish this task, the research question was set as "Does winning the MBNQA have a significant effect on a ROA?" In order to better answer this question, two hypotheses and two null hypotheses were identified. The first hypothesis indicated that winning the MBNQA award would have a statistically significant effect on the organization's return on equity, indicating the organization would have increased, definite, and noticeable positive results as a direct result of winning the MBNQA. The second hypothesis indicated that winning the MBNQA would have a statistically significance on the ROA of the organization, and the organization would have increased, definite, and noticeable positive results as a direct result of winning the MBNQA. The null hypotheses identified for the study included there would be no difference in company performance before and after winning a MBNQA.

There were certain delimitations of the study, reducing the number of firms studied to those that had data published on them in regard to the winning of the award, and reducing the number of firms to only those who had won the award. Further delimitations included the exclusion of educational services from the study and keeping the study to manufacturing, for-profit firms, and healthcare firms.

The terms were defined and the significance of the study was discussed, indicating the study would have a great significance to those within the field of academics and management, allowing for study of phenomena to continue while providing helpful information to those in management who would like to aid their companies in excelling in the manner indicated by winners of the MBNQA.

Chapter Two served as a means of reviewing relevant literature on the matter, discussing the various studies that had previously been completed in the domain of the MBNQA, allowing for the necessary and relevant background information to be present that would aid in understanding the results gathered, and would aid in an analysis of the results received as a result of the completed study. Data contained therein included a review of the concept of quality management, the award itself, the benefits of the award, and the investments that companies have made in terms of seeking attainment of the award. Further information was provided on the concept of organizational performance as it relates to the award criteria for the obtainment of the award, including the realm of performance excellence (Peng & Prybutok, 2014; Priester & Wang, 2010; Lee & Ooi, 2014; Verhoef & Leeflang, 2009; Wang, 2013). Information regarding the dilemmas and criticisms associated with the awarding of the MBNQA were discussed. The concept of quality management as it related to the performance of the firm and how it affected performance of the firm were discussed, and quality control practices and quality standards were reviewed conceptually, by definition, and by application.

Chapter Three was used as a means of discussing the methodology of the study, the research design, research strategy, philosophy, methods, and sampling. Chapter Four offered a presentation of results of the study. It was made clear that each of the different organizations, prior to entering into competition for the award, made direct and noticeable changes to their practices and policies, allowing the organization to improve its overall performance prior to receipt of the award, with the award serving as confirmation of those changes and increased performance. Antecedents to winning the MBNQA were described, based on the analysis of data, as increased market share, increased revenue, improved sales, and an increased ROA (Cazzell & Ulmer, 2009; Choi et al., 2009; Garvin, 1991; NIST, 2002; Jacob et al., 2004; Mena & Hult, 2009; Scaraboto, 2009; Verhoef & Leeflang, 2009). Additional antecedents to winning the award included improved customer experience, the positioning strategy of the organization, the organization's capabilities, market orientation, the organization's competitive strategies, and the innovativeness of the organization (Cazzell & Ulmer, 2009; Choi et al., 2009; Garvin, 1991; NIST, 2002; Jacob et al., 2004; Mena & Hult, 2009; Scaraboto, 2009; Verhoef & Leeflang, 2009).

Conclusions

It may be concluded that the resultant positive effects seemingly associated with the winning of the MBNQA by firms, regardless of their industry, are antecedents to the changes that are made by the organization in an effort to prove firm excellence and win the award. The culmination of the receipt of the award, and the resultant increases in stock prices are in line with past research regarding increased quality practices and stock prices (Easton & Jarrell, 1998; Hendricks & Singhal, 2001; Foster, 2007; Howard et al., 2005). As Jacob et al. (2012) indicated, "Award winners do witness an increase in market value," however, it is important to note that the award does not serve to bestow firm excellence, but is instead a recognition of firm excellence, allowing the populace at large to receive additional confirmation of the value of the products or services offered to consumers by the winning organizations, something that appears to have been forgotten in light of the research being done in this area. A review of the data collected on the MBNQA winners served to indicate that firms started to improve their overall quality and performance indicators years, and in some cases, decades, before they ever had the MBNQA bestowed upon them.

Implications for the Study, Data Processing and Analysis

The data were manipulated in Excel and imported into SPSS 22 for analysis. The data were interval level and included the corporate performance measures of ROA, ROE, EVA, and MVA. Measures of central tendency were calculated and examined for all of the companies in the sample, for companies that had not won the MBNQA, and for companies that had won the MBNQA. Following the examination of descriptive statistics on the interval level data, the assumptions of linear regression and dependent samples i test were assessed.

For the linear regressions conducted to test hypothesis 1 and Hypothesis 2 and in the auxiliary analysis, the assumptions of normality, linearity, and homoscedasticity were assessed. To assess the assumption of normality, histograms representing the frequency distribution of the interval level data were created and examined for deviations from a bell-shaped curve. Deviations from a bell-shaped curve were found, and data transformations were attempted to aid in creating the bell shape and meeting the assumption of normality. The interval level data were transformed by taking the square root, natural logarithm, and common logarithm of the original scores. However, the distribution was not improved enough to warrant use of the transformed variables in the analysis.

Findings

The assumptions of linearity and homoscedasticity were created by re-questing scatterplots of the standardized residuals against the standardized predicted values in the SPSS output for each of the linear regressions conducted to test the hypotheses and the auxiliary analysis and then examined for patterns in the distribution of points that formed either a curve or a funnel. The distribution of points did not form a curve, or a funnel and the assumptions of linearity and homoscedasticity were considered met.

The assumption of normality was also assessed for the dependent samples t test that were conducted in the auxiliary analysis. The assumption of normality was assessed by creating and examining histograms representing the frequency distribution of points for the interval level dependent variables for each group in the independent variable. The distribution of points was found to deviate from a bell-shaped curve in every case, but the data transformations did not improve the distributions enough to warrant the use of the transformed variables in the analysis.

Hypothesis 1 and Hypothesis 2 were tested with linear regressions. A simple linear regression was conducted to test Hypothesis 1, which posited that there is not a relationship between winning the MBNQA and firm performance. The dependent variable in the linear regression was the interval level variable representing average ROA during the period 2004-2015 for each of the firms in the dataset. The independent variable in the linear regression was the dichotomous variable representing whether the firm in the dataset won the MBNQA (0 = the firm did not win the MBNQA during the period 2004-2015 and 1 = the firm did win the MBNQA during the period 2004-2015).

If the results of the linear regression were significant at the .05 level, the results were considered statistically significant.

A multiple linear regression was conducted to test Hypothesis 2, which posited that there is not a relationship between the performance indicators of number of employees, the price-to-sales ratio of the firm, and the price-to-sales ratio of the competing firm. The dependent variable in the regression was the interval level variable representing average ROA during the period 2004-2015 for each of the firms in the dataset. The independent variables in the linear regression were the interval level variables representing the number of employees in the firm, the price-to-sales ratio of the firm, and the price-to-sales ratio of the competing firm. If the results of the linear regression were significant at the .05 level, the results were considered statistically significant.

Following the hypothesis testing, an auxiliary analysis of the study data was conducted to further examine the relationship between winning the MBNQA and firm performance. The relationship between winning the MBNQA and the performance measures of ROE, EVA, and MVA were analyzed by conducting three linear regressions. Following these three linear regressions, mean differences in the four measures of firm performance (ROA, ROE, EVA, and MVA) by time period (prior to winning the MBNQA and after winning the MBNQA) were examined by conducting four dependent samples r tests.

To examine the relationship between winning the MBNQA and firm performance as measured by ROE, a linear regression was conducted. The dependent variable in the linear regression was the interval level variable representing average ROE during the period 2004-2015 for each of the firms in the dataset. The independent variable in the linear regression was the dichotomous variable representing whether the firm in the dataset won the MBNQA (0 = the firm did not win the MBNQA during the period 2004- 2015 and 1 = the firm did win the MBNQA during the period 2004-2015). If the results of the linear regression were significant at the .05 level, the results were considered statistically significant.

To examine the relationship between winning the MBNQA and firm performance as measured by EVA, a linear regression was conducted. The dependent variable in the linear regression was the interval level variable representing average EVA during the period 2004-2015 for each of the firms in the dataset. The independent variable in the linear regression was the dichotomous variable representing whether the firm in the dataset won the MBNQA (0 - the firm did not win the MBNQA during the period 2004- 2015 and 1 = the firm did win the MBNQA during the period 2004-2015). If the results of the linear regression were significant at the .05 level, the results were considered statistically significant.

To examine the relationship between winning the MBNQA and firm performance as measured by MVA, a linear regression was conducted. The dependent variable in the linear regression was the interval level variable representing average MVA during the period 2004-2015 for each of the firms in the dataset. The independent variable in the linear regression was the dichotomous variable representing whether the firm in the dataset won the MBNQA (0 = the firm did not win the MBNQA during the period 2004- 2015 and 1 = the firm did win the MBNQA during the period 2004-2015). If the results of the linear regression were significant at the .05 level, the results were considered statistically significant.

To examine whether the performance of the firms in the dataset was improved after winning the MBNQA, four dependent samples i tests were conducted on each of the four measures of firm performance: ROA, ROE, EVA, and MVA. To create the variables that were used in the analyses, ROA, ROE, EVA, and MVA, scores were averaged for the period before winning the MBNQA and for the period after winning the MBNQA. If the results of the dependent samples I tests were significant at the .05 level, the differences in performance prior to winning the MBNQA and after winning the MBNQA were considered statistically significant.

Recommendations

The recommendation that would be made would be to increase the number of studies conducted and then synthesize the total results of all the studies in order to be able to obtain the data desired in this study. This study should have been setup as a meta- analysis, but in order to do so, the smaller studies would need to be conducted first. In order to obtain the requisite information for the conduction of such a meta-analysis, individual studies must first be conducted in which a reduction of the investigation of MBNQA winners should be made even further, to those within a specific industry. An example of this would be to limit the study to only car dealerships, only food product companies, or only health care product manufacturers. Taking this limitation, the next step would be to identify the winners for the same specific time frame as used within this study (i.e., a period of eleven years).

Another recommendation to be made after reviewing the results of this study would be to increase the number of studies that are to be conducted on this particular topic for the purpose of obtaining the data necessary to effectively address the null hypotheses identified for the resolution of this study. The study should be recreated as a meta-analysis of those identified associated component studies, ensuring that the requisite data are available. First, individual studies should be conducted, allowing for a reduction of MBNQA winners to an even smaller sampling, to those within a more specific single industry, as in the case of only computer companies or only those within the car industry.

Summary

Many organizations believe in the authenticity and value of NQAs like the MBNQA (Cazzell & Ulmer, 2009; Hladchencko, 2015). Organizations have the tendency to assume the granting of an award on an organization has a great effect on the financial returns and earnings of the company, leading organizations to spend a large amount of time and money on tactics designed to work to ensure the organization is able to attain such an award. In spite of this, the amount of time and money spent on attempting to receive the award are not a true picture of the organization's performance (Gorelick, 2004; Forma, 2012; Jacob et al., 2004).

The purpose of the study was to demonstrate the importance of understanding the link between the performances of an organization with quality improvement initiatives set forth as requirements for the obtainment of a NQA. Elements of quality were investigated in order to determine whether a company is worthy of the receipt of such an award and the MBNQA is one of the most prestigious awards in this group. There has been increased concern that winning a MBNQA does not serve as a measure of a firm's performance, and that the performance of the firm is not improved by the receipt of the award, rather the striving for the award serves as the means of increasing the firm's overall performance, acting as an antecedent to winning the MBNQA. In other words, there is no clear indication or Convincing evidence that winning the award results in higher performance by the organization (Van der Laan et al., 2009; Sabella et al., 2014).

Conclusions

It may be concluded that the resultant positive effects seemingly associated with winning the MBNQA by firms, regardless of their industry, are antecedent to the changes that are made by the organization in an effort to prove firm excellence and win the award. The culmination of the receipt of the award, and the resultant increases in stock prices are in line with past research regarding increased quality practices and stock prices (Easton & Jarrell, 1998; Hendricks & Singhal, 2001; Foster, 2007; Howard et al., 2005). As Jacob et al. (2012)

indicated, "Award winners do witness an increase in market value," therefore, it is important to note the award does not serve to bestow firm excellence, but is instead a recognition of firm excellence, allowing the populace at large to receive additional confirmation of the value of the products or services offered to consumers by the winning organizations, something that appears to have been forgotten in light of the research being done in this area. A review of the data collected on the MBNQA winners served to indicate that firms started to improve their overall quality and performance indicators years, and in some cases, decades, before they ever had the MBNQA bestowed upon them. Thus, the answer to the question of whether winning the MBNQA results in an improved ROA for the organization may be stated to be affirmative. However, it must be staled that winning the MBNQA is not an effective tool for the advancement of the organization as indicated in the intent of the award. It is the attempt to win the award that is the reason for the advancement of the organization itself.

REFERENCES

1988-2007 award recipients' contacts and profiles. (2008). Retrieved from http://www.baldrige.nist.gov/Contacts Profiles.htm

Adam, E. E. (1994). Alternative quality improvement practices and organization performance. Journal of Operations Management, 12{1), 27-44.

Alliance for Performance Excellence. (2008). towe are. Retrieved from http://www.ba1drigepe.org/alliance/who.aspx

Bailey, B. D. (2011). The Malcolm Baldrige National Quality Award process in public higher education institutions and effects on organizational performance: A historical perspective. Retrieved from http://scholars.indstate.edu/bitstream /10484/1853/1/Bailey,%20Bill.PDF

Beard, D. F., & Humphrey, R. L. (2014). Alignment of university information technology resources with the Malcolm Baldrige results criteria for performance excellence in education: A balanced scorecard approach. Journal of Education for Business, 89(7), 382-388. doi: 10.1080/08832323.2014.916649

Beattie, K. R., & Sohal, A. (1999). Implementing ISO 9000: A study of its benefits among Australian organizations. Total Quality Management, 10(1), 95-106. doi: 10.1080/0954412998090

Becker, F. (1990). The total workplace. New York, NY: Van Nostrand Reinhold.

Bell, M., & Omachonu, V. (2011). Quality system implementation process for business success. International Journal of Quality & Reliability Management, 28(7), 723-734. doi: 10.1108/02656711111150814

Berber, N., Pasula, M., & Radosevié, M. (2012). Economic value added in function of determining incentive compensation systems. Engineering Economics, 23{4), 414-424

Biddix, J. (2014). Instrument, Validity, Reliability. Research Rundowns. Retrieved 4 August 2015, from https://researchrundowns.wordpress.com/quantitative- methods/instrument-validity-reliability/

Blankenship, D. (2009). Applied research and evaluation methods in Recreation. Champaign, IL: Human Kinetics.

Bogdan, R. C., & Biklen, S. K. (1992). Qualitative research methods for education. Boston, MA: Allyn & Bacon.

Bourne, M., & Neely, A. (2003). Implementing performance measurement systems: A literature review. Business Performance Management, 5(1), 1-24. doi: 10.1504 /IJBPM.2003.002097

Bowerman, B. L., & O'Connell, R. T. (2003). Business statistics in practice (3'd ed.). Boston, MA: McGraw Hill Irwin.

Brigham, E., & Ehrhardt, M. (2013). Financial management: Theory & practice. Mason, OH: Cengage Learning.

Brooks, R. (2005). Measuring university quality. The Review of Higher Education, 29{l), 1-21. doi: 10.1353/rhe.2005.0061

Calhoun, C. (2002). Opening remarks: Roundtable on rethinking international studies in a changing global context. Items and Issues, 3(3-4), 1.

Campbell, J. Y., &, Shiller, R. J. (1986). Stock returns and the term structure. Journal of Financial Economics 18(2), 373-399. doi: 10.1016/0304-405X(87)90045-6

Cargi11.com. (2015). Cargill Kitchen Solutions. Retrieved 13 July 2015, from http://www.cargi11.com/company/businesses/cargi11-kitchen-solutions/index.jsp

Cazzell, B., & Ulmer, J. M. (2009). Measuring excellence: A closer look at Malcolm Baldrige National Quality Award winners in the manufacturing category. Journal of Technology Management & Innovation, 4{1), 134-142. doi: 10.4067/S0718-27242009000100012

Choi, P., Garcia, R., & Friedrich, C. (2009). Under what circumstances conditions can coopetition develop? An investigation into coopetition formation. Chicago, IL: American Marketing Association

Chong V. K., & Rundus, M. J. (2004). Total quality management, market competition and organizational performance. The British Accounting Review, 36{2), 155 -172. doi: 10.1016/j.bar.2003.10.006

Chow-Cua, M., Goh, T. B., & Wan, T. B. (2003). Does ISO 9000 certification improve business performance? The International Journal of Quality & Reliability Management, 20(8/9), 936-953. doi: 10.1108/02656710310493643

Clegg, J., & Slife, B. D. (2009). Research ethics in the postmodern context. In D. M. Mertens & P. E. Ginsberg (Eds.), The handbook of social research ethics (pp. 23-38). London, UK: Sage.

Cooper, D. R., & Schindler, P. S. (2003). Business research methods (8^ ed.). Boston, MA: McGraw Hill.

Creswell, J. W. (2003). Research design: Qualitative, quantitative, and mixed approaches (2nd ed.). Thousand Oaks, CA: Sage.

Creswell, J. W. (2005). Educational research: Planning, conducting, and evaluating quantitative and qualitative research (2°d ed.). Upper Saddle River, NJ: Merrill.

Creswell, J. W. (2008). Educational research: Planning, conducting, and evaluating quantitative and qualitative research (3r ed.). Upper Saddle River, NJ: Merrill.

Creswell, J. W. (2013). Qualitative inquiry and research design. Choosing among the five approaches (3'd ed.). Thousand Oaks, CA: Sage.

Curkovic, S., Melnyk, S., Calantone, R., & Handfield, R. (2000). Validating the Malcolm Baldrige National Quality Award framework through structural equation modelling. International Journal of Production Research, 38{4), 765 -791. doi: 10.1080/002075400189149

Denzin, N. K. (1989). The research act (3'd ed.). Englewood Cliffs, NJ: Prentice Hall. Doane, D. P., & Seward, L. E. (2007). Applied stati5ti€S ff2 business and economics. Boston, MA: Hill Irwin.

Duarte, N. T., Goodson, J. R., & Arnold, E. W. (2013). Performance management excellence among the Malcolm Baldrige National Quality Award winners in health care. The Health Care Manager, 32{4), 346-358. doi: 10.1097/HCM.0b013e3182a9d704

Duarte, N. T., Goodson, J. R., & Dougherty, T. M. P. (2014). Managing innovation in hospitals and health systems: Lessons from the Malcolm Baldrige National Quality Award winners. International Journal of Healthcare Management, 7(1), 21-34. doi: 10.1179/2047971913Y.0000000052

Dyer, C. (2006). Research in psychology: A practical guide to methods and statistics. New York, NY: Wiley.

Easton, G. S., & Farrell, S. L. (1998), The effects of total quality management on corporate performance: An empirical investigation. The Journal of Business, 71(2), 253-306. doi: 10.1086/209744

Efficiency. (n.d.). In Merriam-Webster's online dictionary. Retrieved from http://www.merriam-webster.com/dictionary/efficiency

Eisenhardt, K. M. (1989). Agency theory: An assessment and review. Academy of Management Review, 14(1), 57-74.

Eisenhardt, K. M., & Graebner, M. E. (2007). Theory building from cases: opportunities and challenges. Academy of Management Journal, SP(1), 25-32. doi: 10.5465/AMJ.2007.24160888

Epstein, M. J., & Hanson, K. 0. (2005). The accountable corporation: Corporate governance (Vol. 1). Retrieved from http://0-ebooks.greenwood.com. novacat.nova.edu/reader.jsp?x=C8492&p=171&bc=EC8 492

Fama, E. F. (1995, January/February). Random walks in stock market prices. Financial Analysis Journal, 55-59.

Foma, E. (2012). Talking of Malcolm Baldrige National Quality Award. Review of Integrative Business & Economics, I(2), 223-230. Form 10-K. (2006). Retrieved from http://www.sec.gov/answers/form10k.htm Foster, S. T. (2007). Does six sigma improve performance? The Quality Management Journal, 14{4), 7-21.

Fowler, F. (2009). Survey research methods. Thousand Oaks, CA: Sage.

Franco-Santos, M., Kennerley, M., Micheli, P., Martinez, V., Mason, S., Marr, B., ... & Neely, A. (2007). Towards a definition of a business performance measurement system. International Journal of Operations & Production Management, 27(8), 784-801.

Galvin, D. A. (1991). Quality on the line. Harvard Business Review, 61{4), 66-75. Garvin, D. A. (1991). How the Baldrige Award Really Works. Harvard Business Review, 80-93. Gasson, S. (2004). Qualitative field studies. In M. E. Whitman & A. B. Woszczynski (Eds.), The handbook of information systems research (pp. 79-102). Hershey, PA: Idea Group.

GEM Council. (2008). Retrieved August 2, 2008, from Global Excellence Model Council Web site: http://www.excellencemodels.org/ExcellenceModels/tabid/53/Default.aspx

Glaser, B. S., & Strauss, A. (1971). The discovery of grounded theory. New York, NY: Aldine.

Global Excellence Model Council Awards. (2005). Retrieved September 28, 2008, from Global Excellence Model Council Web site: http://www.excellencemodels .org/Awards/tabid/54/Default.aspx

Goetz, J. P., & LeCompte, M. D. (1984). Ethnography and qualitative design in educational research (Vol. 19). Orlando, FL: Academic Press.

Gorelick, D. (2004). Putting meaning into the q word. American Printer. Retrieved from http://digital-edition.americanprinter.com/how-to /printing cutting meaning word/

Gottlieb, K. (2015). Southern central foundation recognized for inspirational leadership. Retrieved from http://www.baldrigepe.org/foundation/

Griffith, J. R., Fear, K. M., Lammers, E., Banaszak-Holl, J., Lemak, C. H., & Zheng, K. (2012). A positive deviance perspective on hospital knowledge management: Analysis of Baldrige Award recipients 2002-2008. Journal ofHealthcare Management, 58(3), 187-203.

Groebner, D. F., Shannon, P. W., Fry, P. C., & Smith, K. D. (2005). Business statistics: A decision-making approach. Upper Saddle River, NJ: Pearson Prentice Hall.

Guba, E. G., & Lincoln, Y. S. (1989). Fourth generation evaluation. Newbury Park, CA: Sage.

Haddad, F. S. (2012). The Relationship between economic value added and stock returns: Evidence from Jordanian banks. International Research Journal of Finance and Economics, 89, 6-14.

Harrison, M. I. (1994). Diagnosing organizations: Methods, models, and processes (2"d ed.). Thousand Oaks, CA: Sage.

Health, R. L. (1988). Strategic issues management: how organizations influence and respond to public interests and policies. San Francisco, CA: Jossey-Bass.

Health, R. L. (2010). The SAGE handbook of public relations. Thousand Oaks, CA: Sage.

Healy, P. M., Palepu, K. G., & Ruback, R. S. (1992). Does corporate performance improve after mergers? Journal of Financial Economics, 31, 135-175. doi: 10.1016/0304-405X(92)90002-F

Helfert, E. A. (2003). Techniques of financial analysis: A guide to value creation (11th ed.). Boston, MA: Hill Irwin.

Hendricks, K. B., & Singhal, V. R. (2001). The long-run stock price performance of firms with effective TQM programs. Management Science, #7(3), 359-368.

Heras, I., Casadesus, M., & Dick, G. (2002). ISO 9000 certification and the bottom line: A comparative study of the profitability of Basque region companies.

Managerial Auditing Journal, 17(1/2), 72-78. doi: 10.1108 /02686900210412270

Hermès, C. J., Melo, C., & Negräo, C. O. (2008). A numerical simulation model for plate-type, roll-bond evaporators. International journal of Refrigeration, 31{2), 335-347. doi: 10.1016/j.ijrefrig.2007.05.005

Higgins, R. C. (2007). Analysis for financial management (8* ed.). Boston, MA: Hill Irwin.

Hladchenko, M. (2015). Balanced scorecard: A strategic management system of the higher education institution. International Journal of Educational Management, 29{2), 167-176. doi: 10.1108/ijem-11-2013-0164

Hodder, I. (1994). Theoretical archaeology: A reactionary view. In S. M. Pearce (Ed.), Interpreting objects and collections (pp. 48-52). London, UK: Routledge.

Hossain, M. M., & Prybutok, V. R. (2014). An empirical investigation of the Malcolm Baldrige National Quality Award framework using causal latent semantic analysis. International Journal of Business Excellence, 7(2), 148-167. doi: 10.1504/IJBEX.2014.059546

Howard, L. W., Foster, S. T., & Shannon, P. (2005). Leadership, perceived team climate and process improvement in municipal government. International Journal of Quality & Reliability Management, 22(8), 769-795. doi: 10.1108 /02656710510617229

Hubbard, I. J., Parsons, M. W., Nelson, C., & Carey, L. M. (2009). Task-specific training: evidence for and translation to clinical practice. Occupational Therapy International, Neuromotor Interventions, 16(3-4), 175-189. doi: 10.1002/oti.275

ISO. (2008). ISO 9000 -Selection and use (4 ed.).

Jacob, R. A., Madu, C. N., & Tang, C. (2004). An empirical assessment of financial performance of Malcolm Baldrige Award Winners. International Journal of Quality & Reliability Management, 21(8), 897-914. doi: 10.1108/02656710410551764

Jacob, R. A., Madu, C. N., & Tang, C. (2012). Financial performance of Baldrige Award winners: a review and synthesis. International Journal of Quality & Reliability Management, 29(2), 233-240. doi: 10.1108/02656711211199937

Kafetzopoulos, D., Gotzamani, K., & Psomas, E. (2013). Quality systems and competitive performance of food companies. Benchmarking: An

International Journal, 20(4), 463-483. doi: 10.1108/BU-08-2011-0065

Kaplan, R. S., & Norton, D. P. (1996). The balanced scorecard: Translating strategy into action. Boston, MA: Harvard Business School Press.

Katzer, J., Cook, K. H., & Crouch, W. W. (1998). Evaluating information: A guide for users of social science research (4* ed.). Boston, MA: McGraw Hill.

Kennedy, C. (1988). Evaluation of the management of change in ELT projects. Applied Linguistics, 9(4), 329-342. doi: 10.1093/applin/9.4.329

Kerzner, H. R. (2010). Project Management-Best Practices: Achieving Global Excellence (Vol. 14). New York, NY: John Wiley & Sons.

Kotler, P. (2000). Future markets. Executive Excellence, I Z(2), 6.

Kotter, J. P. (2012, November). Accelerate! A new system that allows the traditional hierarchy to operate in concert with a companywide "strategic network" holds the key to nimble change. Harvard Business Review, 46-58.

Kuzel, A. J. (1992). Sampling in qualitative inquiry. In B. F. Crabtree & W. L. Miller (Eds.), Doing qualitative research: Research methods for primary care (Vol. 3.,'pp. 31-44). Newbury Park, CA: Sage.

Latham, J., & Vinyard, J. (2009). Organization diagnosis, design, and transformation. Hoboken, NJ: John Wiley & Sons.

LeCompte, M. D., & Preissle, J. (1993). Ethnography and qualitative design in educational research (2' d rev. ed.). New York, NY: Academic Press.

Lee, V. H., Ooi, K. B., Chong, A. Y. L., & Seow, C. (2014). Creating technological innovation via green supply chain management: An empirical analysis. Expert Systems with Applications, 41(16), 6983-6994.

Leedy, P. D., & Ormrod, J. E. (2005). Practical research: Planning and design (8* ed.). Upper Saddle River, NJ: Prentice Hall.

Leedy, P. D., & Ormrod, J. E. (2013). Practical research. Planning and design. Boston, MA: Pearson.

Levin, J., & Fox, J. A. (2000). Elementary statistics for social research (8 ed.). Boston, MA: Allyn.

Lincoln, Y. S., & Guba, E. G. (1985). Naturalistic inquiry. Newbury Park, CA: Sage

Martin-Castilla, J. I., & Oscar, R. (2008). EFQM model: Knowledge governance and competitive advantage. Journal of Intellectual Capital, 9(1), 133-156.

Martinez-Costa, M., & Martinez-Lorente, A. R. (2007). A triple analysis of ISO 9000 effects on company performance. International Journal of Productivity and Performance Management, 56(5/6), 484-499. doi: 10.1108 /17410400710757150

Maxwell, J. A. (1992). Understanding and validity in qualitative research. In A. M. Huberman & M. B. Miles (Eds.), The Qualitative Researcher's companion, (pp. 37-64). Thousands Oaks, CA: Sage.

MBNQA factsheet. (2007, November 20). Retrieved August 2, 2008, from http://www.nist.gov/public affairs/factsheet/mbnqa.htm

Medrad, Inc. (2015). Medrad, Inc.: Private Company Information. Bloomberg Business. Retrieved 13 July 2015, from http://www.b1oomberg.com/research/stocks /private/snapshot.asp? privcapId—31338

Mena, J. A., & Hult, G. T. M. (2009, December). A critical review of the capabilities of market-driven organizations. Paper presented at the American Marketing Association Winter Educators' Conference, Chicago, IL. Retrieved from https://archive.ama.org/archive/AboutAMA/Vo1unteerLeads/Academic SIG/Documents/ Winter%20Ed%202009.pdf

Mertens, D. M. (2010). Transformative mixed methods research. Qualitative Inquiry, 16{6}, 469-474. doi: 10.1177/1077800410364612

Mesa. (2015). MESA Cathodic Protection & Control Solution. Retrieved 13 July 2015, from http://www.mesaproducts.com/Home

MidwayUSA.com. (2015). Shop Shooting Supplies Reloading GunsmithingHunting Gear at Midway USA. Retrieved 13 July 2015, from http://www.midwayusa.com/

Miles, M. B., & Huberman, M. (1994). Qualitative data analysis (2"d ed.). Thousand Oaks, CA: Sage.

Morin, R. A., & Jarrell, S. L. (2001). Driving shareholder value: Value-building techniques for creating shareholder wealth. New York, NY: McGraw-Hill.

Morrow, S. L. (2005). Quality and trustworthiness in qualitative research in counseling psychology. Journal of Counseling Psychology, 52{2}, 250-260. doi: 10.1037/0022-0167.52.2.250

Morse, J. (1989). Qualitative nursing research: A free-for-all? In J. M. Morse (Ed.), Qualitative nursing research: A contemporary dialogue (pp. 14-22). Rockville, MD: Aspen.

Mulford, C. W., & Comiskey, E.E. (2002). The financial numbers game: Detecting creative accounting practices. New York, NY: John Wiley & Sons.

National Institute of Standards and Technology. (2011). Frequently asked questions about Malcolm Baldrige National Quality Award, October. Retrieved from! http://www.nist.gov/public affairs? Factsheet/baldfaqs.htm

National Institute of Standards and Technology/SEMATECH e-Handbook of Statistical Methods. (2006). Retrieved from http://www.itl.nist.gov/div898/handbook/eda/section3/eda35b.htm

Neely, A., Gregory, M., & Platts, K. (2005). Performance measurement system design: A literature review and research agenda. International Journal of Operations & Production Management, 25(12), 1228-1263. doi: 10.1108 /01443570510633639

Neuman, W. L. (2003). The meanings of methodology: Social research methods (5 ed.). Boston, MA: Allyn & Bacon Normality test. (2007). In Minilab 15 StatGuide. State College, PA: MINITAB. NQA stock studies. (2008). Retrieved from http://www.baldrige.nist.gov /Stock Studier.htm

Nulla, Y. M. (2013). The effect of return on assets (ROA) on CEO compensation system in TSX/S&P and NYSE indexes companies. International Journal of scientific & Engineering Research, #(2).

Parkp1ace.com. (2015). New & Used Luxury & Sports Car Dealerships in Dallas-Fort Worth - Park Place - Park Place. Retrieved 13 July 2015, from http://www.parkp1ace.com/

Peng, X., & Prybutok, V. (2015). Relative effectiveness of the Malcolm Baldrige National Quality Award categories. International Journal of Production Research, 53(2), 629-647. doi: 10.1080/00207543.2014.961207

Purina.com. (2015). Pushing Pet Nutrition Forward - PurinaR Pet Food & Products. Retrieved 13 July 2015, from https://www.purina.com/

Priester, C., & Wang, J. (2010). Economic value added. In Financial strategies for the manager (pp. 118-135). Berlin, DE: Springer Berlin Heidelberg.

Ray, K. G. (2010). Mergers and acquisitions. New Delhi, India: PHI Learning.

Risvank. (2010). 7 criteria of the Malcolm Baldrige national quality award [Web log post]. Retrieved from http://www.mightymikerichards.com/2010/11/16/7 -criteria-of-the-malcolm-baldrige-national-quality-award/

Roberts, C. (2010). The dissertation journey.' A practical and comprehensive guide to planning, writing, and defending your dissertation (3'd ed.). Thousand Oaks, CA: Corwin Press.

Rovine, M. J., & von Eye, A. (1991). Applied computational statistics in longitudinal research. Boston, MA: Academic Press.

Sabella, A., Kashou, R., & Omran, 0. (2014). Quality management practices and their relationship to organizational performance. International Journal of Operations & Production Management, J4(12), 1487-1505. doi: 10.1108/IJOPM-04-2013-0210

Sanders, D. H., & Smidt, R. K. (2000). Statistics a first course. Boston, MA: McGraw- Hill.

Scaraboto, D. (2009). Information-based imitation as an alternative link between market orientation and firm performance. Chicago, IL: American Marketing Assoc.

SEC filings & forms (EDGAR). (n.d.). Retrieved from http://www.sec.gov/edgar.shtml
Sharp HealthCare. (2015). Top San Diego Doctors and Hospitals. Retrieved 13 July 2015, from http://www.sharp.com/index.cfm

Sharpe, T., & Koperwas, J. (2003). Behavior and sequential analysis: Principles and practice. Thousand Oaks, CA: Sage.

Sproull, N. L. (2002). Handbook of research methods (2nd ed.). Lanham, MD: Scarecrow Press.

Stern, J. (1993). Value and people management. Corporate Finance, 104, 35-37. Stewart, G. B. (1991). The quest for value. New York, NY: HarperCollins.

Stracke, C. M. (2006). Process-oriented quality management. In J. Pawloski & U. Ehlers, (Eds.), Handbook on quality and standardization in e-learning (pp. 79-96). Berlin, DE: Springer.

Tabachnick, B. G., & Fidell, L. S. (2001a). Computer-assisted research design and analysis. Boston, MA: Allyn & Bacon.

Tabachnick, B. G., & Fidell, L. S. (2001b). Using multivariate statistics (4 ed.). Boston, MA: Allyn & Bacon.

Taylor, J. K. (1990). Statistical techniques for data analysis. Chelsea, MI: Lewis.

The Malcolm Baldrige National Quality Improvement Act of 1987 - Public Law 100-107. (2001, September 25). Retrieved August 2, 2008, from http://www.quality .nist.gov/PDF files/Improvement Act.pdf

To, W. M., Lee, P. K., & Yu, B. T. (2012). Benefits of implementing management system standards: A case study of certified companies in the Pearl River Delta, China. The TQM Journal, 24{I), 17-28. doi: 10.1108 /17542731211191195

Tong, Y., Yao, Y., & Xiong, X. (2010, January). Performance evaluation of logistics enterprises based on economic value added and balanced scorecard. Paper presented at the 2010 IEEE International Conference on Logistics Systems and Intelligent Management, Harbin Heilongjiang, China.

University of Wisconsin. (2011). Malcolm Baldrige Award frequently asked questions. Retrieved from http://www.uwstout.edu/about/mba/faq.cfm#24

US News. (2015). Advocate Good Samaritan Hospital in Downers Grove, IL. Retrieved 13 July 2015, from http://health.usnews.com/best-hospitals/area/i1/advocate -good- samaritan-hospital-6431475
Van der Laan, G., Van Ees, H., & Van Witteloostuijn, A. (2008). Corporate social and financial performance: An extended stakeholder theory, and empirical test with accounting measures. Journal of Business Ethics, 79{3), 299-310.

Van der Stede, W. A., Chow, C. W., & Lin, T. W. (2006). Strategy, choice of performance measures, and performance. Behavioral Research in Accounting, 18, 185-205.

Vance, D. E. (2003). Financial analysis and decision making: Tools and techniques to solve financial problem and make effective business decisions. New York, NY: McGraw-Hill Companies.

Verhoef, P. C., & Leeflang, P. S. H. (2009). Understanding the marketing department's influence within the firm. Journal of Marketing, 73{2}, 14-37. doi: 10.1509 /jmkg.73.2.14

Wang, W., & Fan, Y. (2010, August). Research on EVA based performance measurement in service-oriented enterprise. Paper presented at the 2010 WASE International Conference on Information Engineering, BeiDai, China.

Wang, Z. (2013). Do the investment and return on equity factors proxy for economic risks? Financial Management, 42{I}, 183-209. doi: 10.1111/j.1755- 053X.2012.01212.x

Williams, J., Haka, S. F., Bettner, M. S., & Carcello, J. V. (2006). Financial accounting (12* ed.). Boston, MA: McGraw-Hill/Irwin.

Wilson, D. D., & Collier, D. A. (2000). Empirical investigation of the Malcolm Baldrige national quality award casual model. Decision Sciences, 31{2}, 1-30. doi: 10.1111 /j.1540-5915.2000.tb01627.x

Wilson, J. P., Walsh, M. A., & Needy, K. L. (2003). An examination of the economic benefits of ISO 9000 and the Baldrige Award to manufacturing firms. Engineering Management Journal, 15(4), 3-10.

www.ingramcontent.com/pod-product-compliance
Lightning Source LLC
Chambersburg PA
CBHW060416290526
45791CB00002B/776